T0369875

WRITE! WRITE! WRITE!

WRITE! WRITE! WRITE!

Ready-to-Use Writing Process Activities for Grades 4-8

CAROL H. BEHRMAN

JOSSEY-BASS
A Wiley Imprint
www.josseybass.com

Copyright © 1995 by John Wiley & Sons, Inc. All rights reserved.

Published by Jossey-Bass
A Wiley Imprint
989 Market Street, San Francisco, CA 94103-1741   www.josseybass.com

No part of this publication may be reproduced, stored in a retrieval system, or transmitted in any form or by any means, electronic, mechanical, photocopying, recording, scanning, or otherwise, except as permitted under Section 107 or 108 of the 1976 United States Copyright Act, without either the prior written permission of the Publisher, or authorization through payment of the appropriate per-copy fee to the Copyright Clearance Center, Inc., 222 Rosewood Drive, Danvers, MA 01923, 978-750-8400, fax 978-750-4470, or on the web at www.copyright.com. Requests to the Publisher for permission should be addressed to the Permissions Department, John Wiley & Sons, Inc., 111 River Street, Hoboken, NJ 07030, (201) 748-6011, fax (201) 748-6008, e-mail: permcoordinator@wiley.com.

Permission is given for individual classroom teachers to reproduce the pages and illustrations for classroom use. Reproduction of these materials for an entire school system is strictly forbidden.

Jossey-Bass books and products are available through most bookstores. To contact Jossey-Bass directly call our Customer Care Department within the U.S. at 800-956-7739, outside the U.S. at 317-572-3986 or fax 317-572-4002.

Jossey-Bass also publishes its books in a variety of electronic formats. Some content that appears in print may not be available in electronic books.

Illustrations are reproductions from the fine Dover Press Pictorial Archives series.

Library of Congress Cataloging-in-Publication Data

Behrman, Carol H.
    Write! Write! Write! : Ready-to-use writing process activities for
grades 4–8 / by Carol H. Behrman.
        p.   cm.
        ISBN 0-87628-936-7
        ISBN 0-7879-6582-0 (layflat)
        1. English language—Composition and exercises—Study and teaching
    (Elementary)   2. Language arts (Elementary)   3. Activity programs in
    education.   II. Title.
    LB1576.B428   1995   95-4989
    372.6'23—dc20

FIRST EDITION
PB Printing 10 9 8 7 6 5 4 3 2

Dedication

To Edward

Who Makes It All Possible, As Always—Best Friend,
Best Critic, Best Support, and Inspiration

About the Author

Carol H. Behrman was born in Brooklyn, New York, graduated from City College of New York, and attended Columbia University's Teachers' College, where she majored in education. She married Edward Behrman, an accountant, and moved to Fair Lawn, New Jersey, where they raised three children and where they still reside. For many years, Behrman taught grades five through eight at the Glen Ridge Middle School, where she created a program, utilizing the writing process, that combined language arts with word-processing instruction. She has written eighteen books, fiction and nonfiction, for children and young adults, and has conducted numerous workshops on the writing process for students, teachers, and aspiring writers. She serves as writer-in-residence at Chautauqua Institution and has been an adjunct lecturer at Seton Hall and New York University's Writing Center.

Preface

Most educators will agree that there is no such thing as "too much" writing practice. This workbook is for the teacher who is seeking additional writing experiences for students, geared to their interests as well as to growth in specific writing skills.

We hear laments from businesspeople and college administrators alike. *Why can't our people (or students) write clearly and competently?* The lack is so great that a whole new service industry emerged—writing facilitators who will go into the job place and lead workshops and seminars designed to produce employees who are able to communicate with the written word.

Why should this be necessary, especially in light of the emphasis that has been placed on writing skills throughout school curricula in recent years? Even the widespread use of the writing process, a method with proven success, doesn't appear to have dimmed the outcry for better writing skills in business and higher education.

Many theories have been offered for this problem. There is the pervasive influence of the nonwritten media such as television, film, and radio. It does seem as though *the medium is the message*, as was predicted decades ago by Marshall MacLuhan, and people today are more in tune with visual and aural input. Then there is the corruption of the language into something resembling street English. Fluidity and change in language has always gone on, but there now seems to be more rapid acceptance of these corruptions as valid, especially in verbal communication. Except for those who may read columns and books by linguists like William Safire, there doesn't seem to be much concern about what is or is not correct English usage. This laissez-faire, "anything goes" attitude may work orally in face-to-face (or telephone-to-telephone) conversation, but it can be confusing and ineffective when written. The spoken word can be clarified by expression, vocal inflections, body language, and visual stimuli. The written word depends on structure and clarity of expression. When this is missing, writing degenerates.

Whatever the reason, the problem remains. How can our children learn to write more effectively? As with any other skill, it seems to this teacher and author that once initial instruction in the writing process has been given, drill and more and more practice (especially the kind that is structured and guided) is the key. In order to accomplish this, a wealth of writing activities is required, especially those that will interest students while helping them acquire writing expertise.

Students learn to write by writing. When they acquire confidence in their ability to communicate, writing will begin to seem less like drudgery and more like an exciting, engrossing activity. It is hoped that this workbook will be one tool among many that will "turn students on" to writing.

About This Resource

━━━━━━━▶

This workbook is designed to supplement any writing curriculum or to stand on its own as a resource for additional writing projects. Its primary aim is to provide a variety of easy-to-use activities that will give students the directed practice they need to acquire writing skills.

The motivation for this book and most of the ideas in it arise from the author's own 15 years of experience teaching writing skills to middle school students, an understanding of student needs for a multiplicity of guided writing experiences, and the teachers' requirements for handy, easy-to-use activities that will provide this practice. The reproducible activity sheets in this book can be used for class assignments and are equally effective for students in individualized programs. The primary focus is on mastery of the writing process—prewriting activities, including brainstorming alone or in groups, speedy writing of a first draft, revisions, and the final copy.

While teacher guidance and input is always helpful, the instructions on these worksheets are at the level of student understanding. Students in grades four through eight should have no difficulty completing these activities on their own with a minimum of teacher involvement. The teacher has the option, therefore, of offering these as individual assignments, to be shared in small groups or as teacher-led class activities.

These guided writing activities can build student confidence in themselves as competent writers and dissipate the feelings of being threatened and blocked that are evoked in many boys and girls when confronted with a writing assignment. To this end, the tone of the text and instructions is light, casual, and encouraging.

The initial activities are simple and fun to do. Their goal is to give students a pleasant familiarity with language and the uses of words in varied combinations and situations. The title of this first unit, Playing with Language, indicates its purpose—to help students overcome negative attitudes toward writing and to guide them into thinking of it as pleasure rather than torture. While process writing steps are omitted in this unit, most of the simple activities do have an educational purpose. For example, "Invasion of the Letter Snatchers" is designed to improve editing skills and the ability to spot spelling errors. The purpose of "Batting Champ" is to encourage the use of active verbs. "Fill-in-Stories" are easy-to-do precursors to narration and creative writing. Many teachers find them particularly useful at times when students tend to be restless, such as just before holidays or vacations. It is hoped that the students will be having too much fun to notice the underlying educational goals. The playful aspects of language are emphasized for positive reinforcement.

Subsequent units become more complex, but this is done gradually. By the time the students reach the more difficult projects, they should be fully prepared for them by what has gone before and be confident in their ability to succeed. It is not necessary that every single assignment be completed for this workbook to be effective. Any activity can be useful at any time the teacher perceives it to be applicable to current class needs.

All activities in Units Two through Eight are structured to train students in the specific techniques of competent writing, including sentence and paragraph structure, the framework of an essay, and the use of clear, precise language to convey a desired outcome. This is achieved by guiding the students in the writing process, step by step, and then applying these principles in composing essays, letters, stories, journals, and so on. Emphasis is placed not only on helping students become familiar with the elements of good writing, but also on training them to apply that knowledge to their own work, particularly when revising. Student writers often fail to master the revision process. For too many of them, their post-revision copy differs very little from their first draft. To this end, many of the exercises in this book direct student attention to only one or two elements of good writing at a time and require the student to consider only those aspects when reviewing that particular assignment. As the students accumulate hands-on experience applying these various techniques to their own writing, they should gradually be able to incorporate more and more of them not only into their revised copy but in first drafts as well.

Teaching students to write via the steps of the writing process is no longer a new or faddish concept. Most educators who are involved with writing instruction are familiar with the process. Therefore, it will not be minutely described or analyzed here except to point out its proven effectiveness when used properly. Teachers who wish more details about this method can find many texts available, including the author's own *HOOKED ON WRITING: Ready-to-Use Writing Process Activities for Grades 4-8*, The Center for Applied Research in Education, 1990.

The instructions for each activity are simple, clear, and easy for students to follow with or without teacher guidance. A student who completes all the assignments should be well along the road to mastering the writing process and subsequently be able to use it independently.

These twin aims—to make writing enjoyable and to help the students acquire mastery of the writing process—provide the foundation for all the activities in this workbook, which is organized as follows:

UNIT ONE: Playing With Language—Activities that offer pleasurable and exciting stimulation with words, phrases, and sentences, and give students a positive feeling for language usage. Some of the activities included are fill-in stories, construction of sentences repeating the first letter of each word, projects using similes, metaphors, sensory language, active verbs, synonyms, opposites, and so on.

UNIT TWO: Paragraph Writing—Activities that offer experience in paragraph construction, utilizing the steps of the writing process.

UNIT THREE: Simple Essays—Activities giving instruction and practice in the construction of simple essays, utilizing the steps of the writing process.

UNIT FOUR: More Complex Essays—Same as Unit Three, with more advanced essay subjects and construction, including some business and technical subjects.

UNIT FIVE: Simple Letters—Activities giving instruction and practice in writing simple personal letters, utilizing the steps of the writing process.

UNIT SIX: Business Letters—Activities giving instruction and practice in the construction of business letters, such as job applications, letters of complaint, and sales letters, utilizing the steps of the writing process.

UNIT SEVEN: Creative Writing—Activities giving instruction and practice in writing descriptions, dialogue, characterization, plot, and complete stories, utilizing the steps of the writing process.

UNIT EIGHT: Variety Pack—A variety of writing activities, including journals, personal experiences, journalism, and poetry, utilizing the steps of the writing process.

ADDITIONAL NOTE TO TEACHERS

There is a fairly wide differential in writing readiness and ability of fourth-graders as compared to eighth-grade students. Most of the activities in this workbook are designed to bridge this span. The responses of an average eighth-grader will be quite different from those of a fourth-grade student, but the structure of the activity and the form of the worksheet will be the same. Naturally, teachers' own evaluations of their students' specific needs and interests will guide the choice of worksheets for any particular individual or class.

Contents

Unit Two: Paragraph Writing 33

Unit Three: Simple Essays 71

Unit Four: More Complex Essays 115

Unit Eight: Variety Pack 275

UNIT ONE

Playing With Language

Contrary to what many students believe, writing can be a pleasurable activity. This unit is designed to give boys and girls hands-on experience with language as fun, to increase their comfort level with words and phrases, and to give them a positive feeling for the written word. Although each exercise has some specific purpose for building knowledge of the uses of language, the form and instructions are light, casual, and emphasize the idea of enjoyment rather than dreary drill. This is the only unit in this workbook that does not use any steps of the writing process beyond that of a first draft in its most elemental form.

Name _____   **Date** _____

The Timid Turtle

Fill-In Story

DIRECTIONS: Fill in the blanks with your own words and phrases. Then complete the story, using the back of this paper.

It was a warm day in the month of _____. I was with my friends _____ and _____. We were out in the backyard, tossing around my _____ ball. My friend _____ threw the ball too high and it _____ into some _____ bushes.

"You _____!" I shouted. I ran back and peered through the _____, looking for the ball. I didn't see it, but I did see something else. Something _____! It was a turtle creeping along the _____. The _____ thing had legs, a _____ head, and a _____ shell.

I wanted that _____ turtle! I wanted to be able to show it to my _____ friends. I reached through the _____ and picked up that _____ thing. Holding it in my _____ fist, I ran over to the _____ kids.

"Look!" I said in a _____ voice, and opened my fist.

The turtle's _____ feet and _____ head had disappeared. Only the _____ shell could be seen.

"Wow!" said _____. "Give me that _____ turtle!"

"No way!" I _____ it. "It's my _____!"

_____ grabbed my hand, and the turtle _____. I was so angry that I _____ (Finish this story on the back of this paper.)

© 1995 by John Wiley & Sons, Inc.

Name _____   **Date** _____

The Bully

Fill-In Story

© 1995 by John Wiley & Sons, Inc.

DIRECTIONS: Fill in the blanks with your own words and phrases. Then complete the story, using the back of this paper.

It was _____'s first day in the new school. He felt a little _____. The teachers were _____. The kids seemed _____. It was a _____ day for _____, but at last it was over. The _____ bell rang and _____ rushed outside. At the bottom of the _____ steps, someone blocked his way. The guy was as big as a _____. He had a _____ face with a _____. His arms were _____, and his hands looked like two _____. The look in his eyes was _____.

"What's your name, kid?" he asked in a _____ voice. _____ told the guy his name.

"I'm _____," the _____ guy said. "Give me all the money you got on you, or I'll punch you out."

_____ put his hand in his pocket and pulled out _____ cents. He handed it to the _____, who counted it.

"You better bring _____ more tomorrow, or you'll be _____." The _____ bully shook his _____ fist.

_____ ran all the way home. The next _____ he didn't want to go to school because he was _____ that the kid would pick on him again. But his _____ said he had to go.

That afternoon _____ (Finish this story on the back of this paper.)

Name _____ **Date** _____

A Summer in Space

Fill-In Story

DIRECTIONS: Fill in the blanks with your own words and phrases. Then complete the story, using the back of this paper.

© 1995 by John Wiley & Sons, Inc.

It was the first day of summer vacation in the year 22____. The _____ family was trying to decide where they would go that year in their _____ spaceship. The oldest boy, _____, who was _____ years old, thought it would be a good idea to visit the planet _____. His twin sister, _____, objected.

"My friend _____ went there last year," she said. "She hated it because it was so _____. There were too many _____ there and not enough _____.

"Let's go to _____," suggested seven-year-old _____. "We could _____ and _____ on _____."

"No way!" said _____. "That planet is for _____."

They argued about it for _____ hours. Finally, they decided to take a trip to _____. They packed their _____ and their _____ and climbed into the _____ spaceship. Before taking off, they stopped at the fuel station on _____ Street and filled up with enough _____ for the _____ mile journey. Then they went to the lift-off point at _____ and zoomed away.

In the spaceship, they ate _____ and _____ and took turns _____. It was a _____ trip. Finally, after a journey of _____ days, they arrived at _____. When they got out of the spaceship, the first thing they saw was _____. (Continue this story in your own words. Use the back of this paper.)

4

Name _____ **Date** _____

A Thanksgiving Meal
Fill-In Story

DIRECTIONS: Fill in the blanks with your own words and phrases. Then complete the story, using the back of this paper.

Robbie _____ had a pet turkey. The turkey was _____

_____ and _____. It lived in a _____ behind

Robbie's house. Robbie _____ his turkey. Robbie's

_____ had given him the turkey for _____. Robbie

took care of the turkey. He fed it _____ times a _____. The turkey liked

to eat _____ and _____.

By November, the turkey had grown _____ and _____.

One _____ day, Robbie's mother said, "Next _____ will be

Thanksgiving. We'll need a _____ turkey for Thanksgiving dinner."

Robbie stared at her with a _____ look on his face. Surely, she didn't

plan to _____ his pet turkey! Robbie was _____.

"They're selling _____ turkeys at the _____ market," he

told his mother.

She shook her head _____. "We don't have enough money to buy a turkey."

Robbie worried about his _____ turkey all day. He couldn't finish

dinner, even though they had his favorite meal, _____. He went out to

the _____ and petted the turkey. "Don't worry, _____," he told

it. "I'll _____ you." But how? Suddenly, Robbie had an idea. He thought of

a _____ to have a _____ Thanksgiving dinner for his family and still

_____ his _____ pet.

Here's what Robbie did. He _____ (Finish this story in your

own words. Use the back of this paper.)

5

Name _____   **Date** _____

Scary Sentences

DIRECTIONS: Write scary sentences in which each word begins with the same letter. The first one is done for you. (You may use small words like *or, on, the,* and *and* that don't start with that letter.)

H Horrible hauntings happen here on Halloween. _____

G _____

S _____

W _____

P _____

J _____

T _____

© 1995 by John Wiley & Sons, Inc.

Name _____   **Date** _____

Colorful Sentences

DIRECTIONS: Write sentences in which each word begins with the same letter as the color. The first one is done for you. (You may use small words like *the, on, or,* and *and* that don't start with that letter.)

Blue Blue belugas bump brave bluish bears. _____

Red _____

Orange _____

Purple _____

Green _____

Yellow _____

Black _____

Grey _____

White _____

© 1995 by John Wiley & Sons, Inc.

Name _____   Date _____

Sensational Similes

DIRECTIONS: A simile compares one thing to something else. The words *like* or *as* are usually used to make the comparison. Can you complete the similes in the following sentences with interesting comparisons?

EXAMPLE: The fisherman's beard was as bushy <u>as a dense forest</u>.

1. The scream was as loud as _____.

2. After three miles, the runner was as tired as _____.

3. The July sun was as hot as _____.

4. Following my brother's directions is like _____.

5. My room at home is like _____.

6. The new girl in class was as quiet as _____.

7. When Joe won the prize, he was as proud as _____.

8. The winter snow is like _____.

9. When I sneezed in class, I felt like _____.

10. The game was as much fun as _____.

11. The old woman was as tiny as _____.

12. Passing that test was as difficult as _____.

13. I ran from that ghost as fast as _____.

14. Susan's sunburn was as red as _____.

15. The stale bread tasted like _____.

16. The small girl looked as sad as _____.

17. The ocean water was as cold as _____.

© 1995 by John Wiley & Sons, Inc.

A Surprise at the Beach

Fill-in Story With Similes

DIRECTIONS: This is a different kind of fill-in story. Fill in all the blanks with similes. A simile compares one thing to something else. The words *like* or *as* are usually used. Some similes are *as scary as a ghost, as tall as a skyscraper,* or *as white as snow.* Can you think up original similes to complete this story?

One Saturday in July, the Smith family decided to go to the beach. The kids, Jimmy and Jennifer, were as excited _____. They took their blankets, beach balls, and lunch baskets and piled into their small car. It was as crowded as _____.

"Stop poking me," said Jennifer. "Your elbow feels like _____."

"And you're as fat as _____," yelled Jimmy.

The kids fought like _____ all the way. But at last they arrived. It was a great day for the beach. The sun was as _____ _____, and the sand was as _____. They spread out their blanket and went into the water, which was cool like _____. The waves were gentle like _____. When they got out of the water, they noticed a group of people looking at something at the other end of the beach. Jimmy and Jennifer were as curious as _____. They ran over as fast as _____. What they saw was as shocking as _____ _____. There on the beach was a group of monsters. They were as large as _____.

"Those monsters look dangerous like _____," said Jimmy.

Jennifer laughed. "Look closer," she said. "They're made of sand."

© 1995 by John Wiley & Sons, Inc.

That's what they were—sand sculptures, but they looked as real as _____. There was a whale, a huge fish, and an alligator. The whale was as _____. The fish looked like _____, and the alligator's teeth looked sharp like _____. The kids went closer and (Finish this story below and on the back of this paper if necessary.)

© 1995 by John Wiley & Sons, Inc.

Name _____ **Date** _____

Opposites Attract

DIRECTIONS: On the line next to each word, write another word that means the opposite.

EXAMPLE: hot <u>cold</u>

1. happy _____   *11.* wrong _____

2. inside _____   *12.* different _____

3. difficult _____   *13.* beautiful _____

4. strong _____   *14.* best _____

5. early _____   *15.* old _____

6. fast _____   *16.* expensive _____

7. war _____   *17.* crooked _____

8. good _____   *18.* hate _____

9. awake _____   *19.* first _____

10. clever _____   *20.* worst _____

© 1995 by John Wiley & Sons, Inc.

© 1995 by John Wiley & Sons, Inc.

Name _____ Date _____

Extended Opposites

DIRECTIONS: Single words aren't the only way to express opposites. Sometimes whole phrases (groups of words) can be opposite to each other. On the line next to each phrase, write a phrase (two or more words) that means the opposite. There can often be several choices, as in the example below, but you need to choose only one.

EXAMPLE: a tall man   <u>a short man (or) a short woman</u>

1. end of summer   _____

2. down below   _____

3. run up the stairs   _____

4. lose the war   _____

5. a sunny day   _____

6. a full glass   _____

7. a loud shout   _____

8. a friendly hello   _____

9. a difficult question   _____

10. a small, dark room   _____

11. a cowardly fellow   _____

12. hold tightly   _____

13. my left arm   _____

14. a cruel stranger   _____

15. laugh happily   _____

Name _____ **Date** _____

Contrary Mary

DIRECTIONS: "Don't be so contrary." Do people sometimes say that when you insist on the opposite of what they've just said? Well, here's your chance to be as contrary as you like! In fact, the more opposites you can come up with, the better!

Read the following story. Then, copy the story in the space below, changing it by using the opposites of as many words as you can.

EXAMPLE: You might change the first sentence from "<u>A long time ago, a large house stood on the north corner of Upper Main Street</u>" to "<u>A short time ago</u> (or <u>recently</u>), <u>a small house stood on the south corner of Lower Main Street</u>."

Have fun and don't forget to be very contrary!

A long time ago, a large house stood on the north corner of Upper Main Street. A big, happy family lived there. The eldest daughter was named Roberta. She had a beautiful room on the top floor. Roberta's room was very neat. Her mom said, "Roberta, you are good. You have the cleanest and neatest room in this house." One cold, winter day, the family went shopping. While they were gone, a kid from next door went into the house. His name was Mike, and he saw Roberta's beautiful room and decided to rest there. Roberta came home and found Mike asleep in her room. "Get out!" Roberta screamed loudly. "A filthy thing like you should not be in my clean room!" Mike was afraid of Roberta. He ran out of her beautiful room and out of the large house as fast as he could. He never came back again.

Now write your contrary (opposite) story below. (Use the back of this paper if you need more room.)

_____

_____

_____

_____

_____

_____

© 1995 by John Wiley & Sons, Inc.

Name _____ **Date** _____

Batting Champ

DIRECTIONS: Baseball is fun and exciting because there is a lot of action. Writing can be fun when you use action words (verbs). Some action words are more exciting than others. For example, *stare, glare, squint,* or *peer* are all more interesting than plain old *see*. And *go* doesn't compare to *rush, hurtle, scamper,* or *slither.*

Sports announcers and sportswriters like to use colorful verbs when describing a game. If you were announcing a ball game, could you find more interesting verbs to use than those in the sentences below?

Rewrite each sentence on the line below, changing the underlined verb to a more exciting action word. Have fun and hit a homerun with your writing!

© 1995 by John Wiley & Sons, Inc.

EXAMPLE: The third baseman <u>picked up</u> the ball.
<u>The third baseman scooped up the ball</u>.

1. The pitcher <u>looked at</u> the batter.

_____

2. The pitcher <u>threw</u> the ball.

_____

3. The batter <u>hit</u> the ball into left field.

_____

4. The outfielder <u>got</u> the ball.

_____

5. The runner on second base <u>went</u> to third.

_____

6. The umpire <u>said</u> "Safe!"

_____

7. The second baseman <u>spoke</u> to the umpire.

_____

8. Another batter <u>went</u> to the plate.

_____

9. This time the ball was <u>hit</u> into the stands for a homerun.

_____

© 1995 by John Wiley & Sons, Inc.

Name _____ **Date** _____

Buried Treasure

DIRECTIONS: Many words have other words hidden inside. If you look carefully at the word *feel,* you can see two other words inside—*fee* and *eel.* If you scramble some of the letters, you can also find *flee* inside the word *feel.*

It's time to go on a treasure hunt! Next to each word below, write down all the hidden words you can find inside. You may scramble the letters to find more words.

How many treasures (hidden words) can you find? When you finish, add up all the words you located and write down your total number of treasures. It could be fun to compare your total treasures with your classmates. Did they find any words you missed? Maybe you discovered some treasures they didn't.

Good luck!

EXAMPLE: feel   <u>fee, eel, flee</u>

1. snow   _____
2. winter   _____
3. these   _____
4. please   _____
5. price   _____
6. stair   _____
7. steam   _____
8. heart   _____
9. small   _____
10. stick   _____
11. shame   _____
12. hours   _____
13. drink   _____
14. teacher   _____
15. tables   _____

Treasure count—write your total words here _____

Name _____   Date _____

Invasion of the Letter Snatchers

In the classic sci-fi movie called *Invasion of the Body Snatchers,* aliens take over the bodies of Earth people. In this activity, you are going to search for alien letters that are trying to take over words. You must stop them and save the English language from these invaders!

DIRECTIONS: Each of these words contains an alien letter. Can you find this alien letter and replace it with the letter that really belongs? Write the real word on the line next to each alien takeover.

EXAMPLES: sciense   <u>science</u>   diel   <u>dial</u>

1. screem _____

2. plase _____

3. becouse _____

4. phraze _____

5. importent _____

6. elephint _____

7. docter _____

8. voluntear _____

9. populer _____

10. porselain _____

11. challange _____

12. dictionery _____

13. messege _____

14. pleaze _____

15. pockit _____

16. leed _____

17. simalar _____

18. uncleer _____

19. posative _____

20. differant _____

21. motorcycle _____

22. leep _____

23. soccor _____

24. celabrate _____

© 1995 by John Wiley & Sons, Inc.

Name _____ **Date** _____

All Through The Year

DIRECTIONS: Each month of the year has its own special quality—holidays, events, weather, games, and celebrations—that makes that month unique.

　　Next to each month, write as many words or phrases you can think of that pertain to that month. January has been started for you, but you can surely add many more for January and all the months that follow.

　　Have a wonderful year!

January New Year's Day, snow, _____

February _____

March _____

April _____

May _____

June _____

July _____

August _____

September _____

October _____

November _____

December _____

© 1995 by John Wiley & Sons, Inc.

Name _____   **Date** _____

Memorable Months

DIRECTIONS: Next to each month, write one or two sentences describing that month. Use some or all of the ideas you came up with in "Activity 15A: All Through the Year."

January _____

_____

February _____

_____

March _____

_____

April _____

_____

May _____

_____

June _____

_____

July _____

_____

August _____

_____

© 1995 by John Wiley & Sons, Inc.

September _____

_____

October _____

_____

November _____

_____

December _____

_____

© 1995 by John Wiley & Sons, Inc.

Dr. Healthy Needs You!

Dr. Healthy gives out words instead of medicine. Some of his words make you feel good. Others may make you feel terrible. The important thing is that these special words make the reader feel something! That's because they appeal to the senses.

These *sensory words* usually refer to one of the five senses—taste, touch, sight, sound, or smell. Dr. Healthy's problem is that he's running out of sensory words. He needs assistants who can supply more.

Each of the five senses has its own medicine box below. Only a few words are left in each box. Can you fill up these boxes with sensory words? Dr. Healthy and his reader-patients will be grateful.

DIRECTIONS: Fill up the boxes with as many sensory words as you can. Some words can be used for more than one sense. For instance, *sharp* could refer to touch as well as taste.

TASTE

peppery, nutty, sweet,

TOUCH

rough, icy, soft,

SIGHT

blue, dark, bright,

SOUND

whisper, ring, bang,

SMELL

putrid, spicy, sharp,

© 1995 by John Wiley & Sons, Inc.

Name _____   Date _____

Working for Dr. Healthy

Dr. Healthy is happy with all the sensory words you gave him in "Activity 16A: Dr. Healthy Needs You!" You did such a good job that he wants to train you to be his special assistant. He now has all the sensory words he needs, but his special "healthy" medicine needs more. The sensory words need to be combined into sentences to work for his reader-patients. He wants you to do this job for him. Then you can become the new Dr. Healthy.

DIRECTIONS: Under each sense heading, write two sentences. Each sentence should contain at least one of the sensory words on the previous activity sheet. The more sensory words you can include in each sentence, the more potent that "healthy medicine" will be.

EXAMPLE (under "smell"): <u>That mouth-watering, spicy smell made me rush into the aromatic kitchen.</u>

TASTE

1. _____

2. _____

TOUCH

1. _____

2. _____

SIGHT

1. _____

2. _____

SOUND

1. _____

2. _____

SMELL

1. _____

2. _____

© 1995 by John Wiley & Sons, Inc.

Name _____   Date _____

Icky Squirmy

Sensory words can make us really feel, hear, see, taste, or smell what something is like. They can be lots of fun to use in descriptions.

DIRECTIONS: In the box next to each word, write all the sensory words that object brings to mind. Then, on the line below, write a sentence that describes that object. Include sensory words that work best in that one-sentence description.

EXAMPLE: Turtle

> shy, green, hard shell, wet,

My shy green turtle thinks it can't be seen when it hides in its shell.

Worm

Stuffed bear

Spaghetti

Fresh-caught fish

Rock band

Ocean

Football stadium

© 1995 by John Wiley & Sons, Inc.

© 1995 by John Wiley & Sons, Inc.

Name _____ Date _____

How to Build Better . . .

Some builders construct better houses than others. One house may be quite ordinary. Another might be interesting and exciting.

Like a builder, you can make your writing more interesting and exciting by the way you build your sentences. Compare these two sentences:

The man looked at his brother's house.

The jealous, greedy man looked enviously at his rich brother's big house.

Isn't the second sentence much more interesting and exciting? It's done with the use of descriptive words, mainly adjectives and adverbs. Adjectives are the words that describe a noun (person, place, or thing). Adverbs modify verbs. In the second sentence above, the words *jealous* and *greedy* are adjectives that describe the noun *man*. The adjective *rich* describes *brother*. *Enviously* is an adverb that makes the verb *looked* more interesting. You, too, can build more exciting sentences.

DIRECTIONS: Rewrite each sentence on the line below, making it more exciting by adding adjectives and adverbs.

1. The batter faced the pitcher.

_____

2. The boy ran from the room.

_____

3. The student walked to school.

_____

4. The soldier grabbed his rifle.

_____

5. The alien landed in his spaceship.

_____

6. A crowd gathered around the scene of the accident.

_____

7. Her friends came to the party.

_____

Name _____ Date _____

A, My Name Is

Writing or reciting something in which all or most words begin with the same letter is called *alliteration*.

There is a traditional game played on the streets of towns and cities. A player bounces a ball and recites, "A, my name is Alice, my boyfriend's name is Adam, we live in Atlanta, and we eat apples." The same formula is then followed with B, C, and all the letters of the alphabet. It's fun! In this activity, you're going to play the same sort of alliteration game with parts of sentences.

A simple sentence has a subject, a verb, and an object.

The alligator ate an artichoke.

In this sentence, the subject is *alligator*, the verb is *ate*, and the object is *artichoke*. We can add adjectives and adverbs to make the sentence more interesting:

The ancient alligator avidly ate an awful artichoke.

The adjective *ancient* modifies the subject noun *alligator*. The adjective *awful* modifies the object noun *artichoke*. The adverb *avidly* modifies the verb *ate*.

DIRECTIONS: Most of the words in the example begin with the letter A. Can you write sentences where the subjects, objects, and verbs all begin with the same letter? It will be even better if you add adjectives and adverbs beginning with that letter. (You may use occasional small words such as *the, or, a,* and *of* if needed for your sentences.) On the line following each letter below, write alliterative sentences using that letter.

A _____

B _____

C _____

D _____

E _____

F _____

G _____

H _____

I _____

J _____

K _____

© 1995 by John Wiley & Sons, Inc.

Name _____   **Date** _____

Additional Alliteration

DIRECTIONS: On the previous worksheet, you wrote alliterative sentences for letters A through K. Here, you'll do the same for the rest of the alphabet. Remember, the subject, verb, and object must all begin with the same letter. It will be even more fun if you can add adjectives and adverbs beginning with that letter. If necessary, you may use small supportive words such as *the, for, a,* and *of.*

Your sentences can be serious or silly, just as long as they are alliterative. Remember, we want wonderful, wise, and whimsical words!

(Note: Don't worry if you have problems with letters such as X. Most people do.)

L _____

M _____

N _____

O _____

P _____

Q _____

R _____

S _____

T _____

U _____

V _____

W _____

X _____

Y _____

Z _____

© 1995 by John Wiley & Sons, Inc.

Name _____ Date _____

Crazy Jingles

Some commercials on TV and radio use a jingly rhyme to help us remember the product. *Oodles of noodles. See the U.S.A. in your Chevrolet.*

Can you make up funky, rhyming jingles for products you use or see? Write a jingle in each of the boxes. You can use any of the products listed, or any others that you may think of. When you finish, it can be fun to share your jingles with your classmates and hear theirs.

Here are some of the products for which you may wish to write jingles:

bran flakes	mini-vans	peanut butter
VCR	stereo	whole wheat bread
apple pies	chocolate bars	lemonade
raspberry tea	motorbike	cable TV
french fries	apple juice	cheddar cheese
tie-dyed shirts	jeans	running shoes
roller skates	baseball mitts	tuna fish

DIRECTIONS: Write a two-line rhyming jingle in each of the boxes below.

© 1995 by John Wiley & Sons, Inc.

Name _____   Date _____

Trains, Planes, and Flying Saucers

DIRECTIONS: There are many different ways of getting from one place to another. Various methods of transportation are listed below. Some are modern, some are old-fashioned, and some are imaginary. But they are all scrambled. Write the unscrambled word next to each scrambled one. Then, on the line below, write a sentence that tells something about this kind of transportation.

EXAMPLE: swing   <u>wings</u>
<u>Angels and birds spread their wings and fly from place to place.</u>

---

1. ristan   _____

---

2. clebicy   _____

---

3. glinfy preact   _____

---

4. sleanirap   _____

---

5. pessiphac   _____

---

6. shore   _____

---

7. dreevoc angow   _____

---

8. skurct   _____

---

9. sub   _____

---

10. emit camineh   _____

© 1995 by John Wiley & Sons, Inc.

Name _____   Date _____

Sounds the Same to Me!

DIRECTIONS: Homonyms are words that sound alike but have different meanings and can be spelled differently.

    Underline the homonym in each sentence. Then, on the line below, write another sentence, using the other spelling and meaning.

EXAMPLE: They ate <u>their</u> dinner.
               <u>There is a homonym in this sentence.</u>

---

1. He wore new shoes.

    _____

2. The wind blew fiercely.

    _____

3. The tortoise raced with the hare.

    _____

4. The dryer wrings the wet clothes dry.

    _____

5. The car will be ready in an hour.

    _____

6. Would you like to go to the movies?

    _____

7. Is the ship on the correct course?

    _____

8. Always do the right thing.

    _____

9. The chess club will meet this afternoon.

    _____

10. He wants to lose weight.

    _____

© 1995 by John Wiley & Sons, Inc.

Name _____ **Date** _____

Accentuate the Opposite

Do you want to turn words into their opposites? Sometimes this can be done by merely adding a prefix to the beginning of the word. Prefixes that are often used to create an opposite meaning are *dis* and *un,* as in *dis*mount or *un*fed.

DIRECTIONS: On the line next to each word, write its opposite, using either the prefix *dis* or the prefix *un.*

EXAMPLES: assemble   <u>disassemble</u>
                     wholesome   <u>unwholesome</u>

1. worthy _____

2. trust _____

3. cover _____

4. hook _____

5. earthly _____

6. skilled _____

7. sociable _____

8. agreeable _____

9. expected _____

10. believe _____

11. advantage _____

12. obey _____

13. credit _____

14. dress _____

15. please _____

16. holy _____

17. roll _____

18. like _____

19. common _____

20. honest _____

© 1995 by John Wiley & Sons, Inc.

Name _____ **Date** _____

That's What I Think!

DIRECTIONS: Your opinion is important! Show what you think by completing each of the sentences below.

1. Friends should always _____

2. The best things in the world to eat are _____

3. Teachers should not _____

4. Teachers should _____

5. Most parents _____

6. I like my parents best when they _____

7. The most important school subjects are _____

8. Tests are _____

9. Boys are often _____

10. Girls are often _____

11. The President of the U.S. should _____

12. People can live in peace if _____

13. Big cities are _____

14. Small towns are _____

15. The best thing about television is _____

16. The worst thing about television is _____

17. Kids should be able to _____

18. Kids should not be able to _____

19. The best age to be is _____

20. The worst age to be is _____

21. Homework is _____

22. It would be nice if _____

23. The best time of the day is _____

© 1995 by John Wiley & Sons, Inc.

© 1995 by John Wiley & Sons, Inc.

Name _____ **Date** _____

Storm Warning

There has just been a big storm. It was so bad that it fouled up the computer on which this page was written. The letters got all mixed up. These words were part of a list about precipitation (different kinds of storms). Now all the words are scrambled.

DIRECTIONS: Unscramble the words in the list of kinds of storms below. Write the correct word on the line next to each scrambled one.

EXAMPLE: romst   <u>storm</u>

1. nari   _____

2. rhowse   _____

3. wons   _____

4. drootan   _____

5. chrainuer   _____

6. noccley   _____

7. zardbliz   _____

8. leets   _____

9. hila   _____

10. phonoty   _____

Name _____ **Date** _____

Creating Critters

DIRECTIONS: Create living creatures (animals, birds, fish, and reptiles) by adding a letter either at the end or at the beginning of each word. Write the name of your critter on the line next to each word.

EXAMPLE: hero   <u>heron</u>

---

1. nail _____

2. are _____

3. ion _____

4. he _____

5. ear _____

6. hale _____

7. do _____

8. at _____

9. el _____

10. ow _____

11. up _____

12. fro _____

13. haw _____

14. an _____

15. be _____

16. ink _____

17. rake _____

18. came _____

© 1995 by John Wiley & Sons, Inc.

UNIT TWO

Paragraph Writing

This unit offers activities that provide practice in paragraph writing, using projects that are amusing, imaginative, and/or that arise from the students' own experiences.

The steps of the writing process that are stressed in this unit are writing first drafts and revising with an emphasis on correct paragraph construction. Mastery of paragraph writing is the cornerstone of most writing. Sometimes the educational system's expectations of a child's ability are too low and fail to challenge. Too often, however, when it comes to writing, we expect children to become proficient on the basis of one or two lessons and a few exercises. Most writing skills require a great deal of drill before they become ingrained into the students' writing habits. Before students can do well in longer and more complex writing assignments, they must be capable of writing a well-structured, coherent paragraph. This unit aims to give students that type of practice with activities that are both fun and goal-oriented, such as narration of personal experiences, outrageous descriptions, and scrambled paragraph sentences. Most activities are divided into several sections for first drafts, revising, and final copy. For the most part, only one or two aspects of good writing are stressed in the revision process of each assignment in addition to correct paragraph construction.

Name _____   Date _____

Scrambled Paragraphs

DIRECTIONS: The six sentences below can be combined into one paragraph. But they are not in the right order! Can you unscramble them and copy them in the right order into a paragraph? The topic sentence should come first, the concluding sentence last, and the other four sentences in a logical order between them.

1. The trip there would be uncomfortable if our car was not air-conditioned.

2. It is fun to spend a hot summer day at the shore.

3. I spend most of the day in the water riding the waves.

4. When we arrive, we spread our blanket on a spot near the ocean.

5. We get home at the end of the day tired, covered with sand, but happy.

6. The hot dogs and soda we buy on the boardwalk have a special flavor.

Write the paragraph on the lines below.

_____

_____

_____

_____

_____

_____

© 1995 by John Wiley & Sons, Inc.

Here are some more scrambled sentences. Can you combine them into a paragraph in the correct order on the lines on the next page?

1. I saw him put a big worm into Susan Barrow's pocket during recess.

2. Everyone heard, including the teacher, and turned to look at Matthew.

3. It was my fault he got punished, but I guess he deserved it.

4. I once got my best friend, Matthew, into big trouble.

5. I asked him what he was doing in a loud voice.

6. Susan put her hand into her pocket and screamed.

_____

_____

_____

_____

_____

_____

_____

_____

© 1995 by John Wiley & Sons, Inc.

Name _____   **Date** _____

More Scrambled Paragraphs

DIRECTIONS: The six sentences below can be combined into one paragraph. But they are not in the right order! Can you unscramble them and copy them in the right order into a paragraph? The topic sentence should come first, the concluding sentence last, and the other four sentences in a logical order between them.

1. The Forman kids have a backyard gym that I'm allowed to use.

2. What kid wouldn't be happy on a street like this?

3. Best of all, my closest friends, Greg and Caitlin, live down the block.

4. Old Mrs. Buford next door gives me oven-warm brownies every day.

5. The greatest people in the world live on my street.

6. The Guarinos on the other side let me play with their puppies.

Write the paragraph on the lines below.

_____

_____

_____

_____

_____

_____

Here are some more scrambled sentences. Can you combine them into a paragraph in the correct order on the lines on the next page?

1. Then daffodils and tulips appear.

2. Everything comes to life in the spring.

3. Green buds come out on the trees.

4. It's such a pretty season.

5. Even before the snow is gone, crocuses poke up their heads.

6. The grass begins to grow.

© 1995 by John Wiley & Sons, Inc.

_____

_____

_____

_____

_____

_____

_____

_____

_____

© 1995 by John Wiley & Sons, Inc.

Name _____ Date _____

So That's What Happened!
First Draft

The paragraph in the example below tells about something that happened to the writer. Read the paragraph and note especially how the first sentences grab the reader's attention and at the same time tell what the paragraph is about. The *topic sentence* tells what the paragraph will be about. The rest of the paragraph describes some details, and the *concluding sentence* brings this short tale to an end.

EXAMPLE: I couldn't believe it! My sister had looked in my diary. She waved it in my face and asked why I had written such mean things about her. I felt terrible. I tried to explain that I was feeling angry when I wrote those things and didn't really mean them. She said I was lying. I told her that she had no right to be reading my personal stuff. She screamed at me and I screamed back at her. It was awful. Finally, I grabbed my diary and took it back to my own room. From now on, I'll keep my personal writings where nobody can find them!

DIRECTIONS: In the space below, write about something that happened to you. Introduce the event in your *first sentence* in an interesting way. Follow with *at least three sentences* describing the incident. Then, conclude in the *last sentence*. (This will be a first draft, so don't worry about getting it perfect. Just put down what comes into your head. Use the back of this paper if you need more room.)

© 1995 by John Wiley & Sons, Inc.

Name _____ **Date** _____

So That's What Happened!
Revising and Writing a Final Copy

DIRECTIONS: Read the paragraph you wrote and think about ways to make it better. Here are some things you can consider to improve it. (Do all your corrections—crossing words out, adding words, and so on—right on the first draft.)

1. Did your first sentence or two tell what the paragraph is about?

2. Was the first sentence interesting enough to make a reader want to continue? Perhaps you can think of an even better way to grab the reader's attention.

3. Does the body of the paragraph clearly tell the details of what occurred? If anything doesn't seem clear, fix it. If you left out anything important, add it.

4. If this is something that happened to you, it becomes more interesting if you show how you felt about it. Do you show this anywhere in your paragraph? If not, put in a sentence that describes your feelings.

5. Does the final sentence bring the event to a conclusion? If not, write an additional sentence that will truly conclude it.

6. Are your sentences all complete? Have you checked in the dictionary for the correct spelling of words you may be unsure about?

Now, rewrite your paragraph in the space below, making all the changes needed. (Use the back of this paper if you need more room.)

_____

_____

_____

_____

_____

_____

_____

_____

© 1995 by John Wiley & Sons, Inc.

Name _____   **Date** _____

Outrageous Descriptions
First Draft

DIRECTIONS: Read the example below of an outrageous description. Then, on the lines below, write the first draft of a one-paragraph outrageous description of your own. It can be a description of a person, an animal, a machine, a game, or anything else. Let your imagination go wild! Be as silly and ridiculous as you like. Be sure to begin with a topic sentence. Follow up with three or four descriptive sentences, and end with a concluding sentence. Don't worry about mistakes—this is just a first draft.

EXAMPLE: Veggy T. Able has a strange appearance. He is as healthy looking as a vegetable garden in summer. His head is perfectly round and green like a cabbage. He has two black olives for eyes, a red-radish nose, and an orange-yam mouth that is always grinning. There are five green bean fingers on each hand and his belly button is a large green pea. If Veggy ever gets hungry, he might eat himself up and disappear completely.

Write the first draft of your outrageous description here. _____

_____

_____

_____

_____

_____

_____

_____

_____

_____

_____

© 1995 by John Wiley & Sons, Inc.

Name _____ Date _____

Outrageous Descriptions
Revising and Writing a Final Copy

DIRECTIONS: Below is the first draft of an outrageous description written by a seventh-grader. On it, the student has indicated how it will be revised. Note how the topic sentence has been made more clear. The second sentence is more vivid when a simile is added. Spelling errors have been corrected and so has a run-on sentence. After you have studied the example, revise your own outrageous description. Is your topic sentence interesting and clear? Are the details exciting? Try to use a simile to make at least one description more vivid. Does your final sentence conclude the description? Use a dictionary to check your spelling.

A new parent-changing machine will soon be available.

EXAMPLE: ~~Here is a machine to change parents~~. It is a large

a *like something from outer space,*
met~~a~~l box with lots of wires and openings. You write down ~~all~~ the

ly
things you would like your parents to do different on a card and

to *T*
drop it in the top slot. the card travels through different parts

of the machine. There is a section for making bedtime later, one

for more TV watching hours, and another for getting rid of ~~all~~

~~those~~ health foods and serv~~e~~ing pizza, hot dogs, and chocolat~~e~~ bars

and you
for dinner. Sneak this box into your parents' room at night,

will have the greatest parents in town.

© 1995 by John Wiley & Sons, Inc.

Now, make corrections on your own first draft and write the final copy here. _____

_____

_____

_____

_____

_____

_____

_____

© 1995 by John Wiley & Sons, Inc.

Name _____   Date _____

Captain Hook
First Draft

Captain Hook is a villainous pirate in *Peter Pan*. Captain Hook uses the deadly hook he has instead of a hand to get attention. You can't ignore Captain Hook!

The first sentence of a paragraph is sometimes called a "hook." It's supposed to grab the reader's attention and make him or her want to keep reading. A boring first sentence is not a successful "hook." A good "hook" must be exciting and interesting.

Here are some examples of boring and interesting first sentences:

© 1995 by John Wiley & Sons, Inc.

EXAMPLES:	Boring—	Our class went on a trip.
	Good "hook"—	You won't believe what happened on our class trip!
	Boring—	Last week, we moved to a new house.
	Good "hook"—	I never thought that moving would be so hard.
	Boring—	This is what happened the first time I baby-sat.
	Good "hook"—	My first baby-sitting job was a total disaster.

DIRECTIONS: Write the first draft of a paragraph on one of the following subjects:

A class trip	My first airplane flight
Moving to a new house	An unusual family
My first job	Getting home late from school
My first attempt to cook	An embarrassing moment

Your paragraph should have at least five sentences: a beginning sentence, a concluding sentence, and a minimum of three sentences in between. Think of Captain Hook when you write the beginning and try to "hook" the reader!

_____

_____

_____

_____

_____

_____

_____

Name _____   Date _____

Captain Hook
Revising and Writing a Final Copy

Think of yourself as Captain Hook when you revise the paragraph you wrote in Activity 32A. Be ruthless! Don't accept defeat! Be sure that your first sentence is a powerful "hook" that will grab your reader and not let go.

DIRECTIONS: First write your revisions directly on your first draft. Give a lot of thought to the first sentence. Is it interesting? Is it a "hook" that would make Captain Hook proud? Can you think of a way to make it even more exciting?

Also examine the rest of the paragraph. Are your sentences clear and complete? Is the information arranged in a logical sequence? Does your concluding sentence sum it up effectively?

Don't guess at spelling. Use the dictionary to check any words that you are unsure of.

When your paragraph is the best it can be, write your final copy below.

_____

_____

_____

_____

_____

_____

_____

_____

_____

_____

_____

© 1995 by John Wiley & Sons, Inc.

Name _____   Date _____

Smooth Sailing
Prewriting

A paragraph should read smoothly like a ship sailing upon a calm sea. If your sentences sound choppy, it may be because they are not flowing smoothly. Sometimes all that is needed is a *transitional* word or phrase. A *transitional word or phrase* connects a sentence to the one that comes before. Some common transitional words and phrases are *however, then, besides, also, therefore, for that reason, nevertheless,* and *on the other hand.*

The pairs of sentences below would seem awkward without the transitions:

I didn't want to go to school because I felt sick. *Besides,* I hadn't completed the homework assignment.

Mark didn't like the Peterson twins. *Nevertheless,* he had to go to their birthday party.

DIRECTIONS: In the sentence combinations below, fill in the blank spaces with transitional words or phrases that connect the sentences more smoothly.

© 1995 by John Wiley & Sons, Inc.

1. Molly thought she saw a ghost. _____, it turned out to be only the shadow of a lamp.

2. Josh couldn't throw a ball well. _____, he didn't want to join the Little League team.

3. Jennie loved hamburgers. _____, the doctor had told her not to eat fried foods.

4. I wanted the dress in the shop window. _____, I didn't have enough money to buy it.

5. Oat bran is a healthy cereal. _____, I don't like the way it tastes.

6. Andrew opened the door. _____ he went into the room.

7. Mrs. Wright is a strict teacher. _____, she gives a lot of homework.

8. We ate dinner at seven o'clock. _____, we cleared the table.

9. Margo's bicycle was broken. _____, she couldn't ride it to her friend's house.

Name _____   Date _____

More Smooth Sailing
First Draft

Transitional words and phrases can make the sentences in your paragraphs flow together more smoothly. In the following assignment, use at least one transitional word or phrase when writing your paragraph.

DIRECTIONS: Write a paragraph about one of these subjects:

a favorite TV show	a TV character I like
a favorite book or story	a person I admire
a strange object in the classroom	a description of my friend
a perfect dinner	a shopping trip

Write the first draft of your paragraph on the lines below. Make your topic sentence interesting. Use an appropriate concluding sentence. Include at least three additional sentences, using at least one transitional word or phrase.

_____

_____

_____

_____

_____

_____

_____

_____

_____

_____

_____

© 1995 by John Wiley & Sons, Inc.

Name _____ **Date** _____

Smooth Sailing
Revising and Writing a Final Copy

DIRECTIONS: Revise the paragraph you wrote for Activity 33B right on the worksheet. Ask yourself the following questions:

1. Is all the spelling correct? (Check with a dictionary if you are not sure.)

2. Can anything be changed to make the topic sentence more exciting?

3. Is there at least one transitional word or phrase connecting sentences to make them flow more smoothly?

4. Are the sentences in a logical order?

5. Are the thoughts clearly expressed? Are there other words or phrases that would express this better?

6. Does the concluding sentence sum up the main idea?

   When you are certain that your revision is as good as it can be, write your final copy on the lines below.

_____

_____

_____

_____

_____

_____

_____

_____

_____

_____

_____

© 1995 by John Wiley & Sons, Inc.

Name _____ Date _____

Looking Good!
Prewriting

It can be fun to write one-paragraph descriptions of people, places, animals, and objects. These are easy to do well if you follow a few suggestions:

1. Don't try to tell everything. A description that goes on and on becomes boring. Choose several facts that seem most important, most typical, most interesting, or most unusual. A few colorful, exciting touches will bring a subject to life more than a lot of boring detail.

2. Choose your descriptive phrases carefully. Create vivid impressions with sensory words, active verbs, and original or startling similes.

3. Introduce your subject in the topic (first) sentence with a "hook" that grabs the reader's interest.

4. Humor can be effective, especially in the topic and concluding sentences. Be careful, however, to avoid cruel humor. This will only turn your reader off. Humor should be subtle and clever or else don't use it at all.

Here is an interesting description:

"Murdstone and Grinby's warehouse was at the water-side. It was the last house at the bottom of a narrow street, curving down hill to the river, with some stairs at the end, where people took boat. It was a crazy old house with a wharf of its own . . . and literally overrun with rats. Its panelled rooms, discoloured with the dirt and smoke of a hundred years . . . its decaying floors and staircase; the squeaking and scuffling of the old grey rats in the cellars; and the dirt and rottenness of the place . . . They are all before me, just as they were in the evil hour when I went among them for the first time."

This is from *David Copperfield* by Charles Dickens. Can't you just see this horrible old house? Note the use of sensory words such as *discoloured, decaying, squeaking,* and *rottenness* that helps the reader to share the experience. Note how the concluding sentence sums up the description in a way that shows how the writer felt about it.

DIRECTIONS: Choose one of the following subjects:

Someone I love	Someone who frightens me
Someone who is funny	An amusing pet
My room	The street on which I live
An imaginary friend	An enemy, real or imaginary

On the back of this worksheet, make the following lists:

1. Four or five main things I want to tell about this subject.

2. A list of sensory words and active verbs I can use about this subject.

3. Two possible topic sentences with hooks.

4. Two possible concluding sentences.

© 1995 by John Wiley & Sons, Inc.

Name _____ **Date** _____

Looking Good!
First Draft

DIRECTIONS:

1. Read once more the descriptive paragraph by Charles Dickens in Activity 34A.

2. Look over your list of the main points about the subject you've chosen. Underline three or four of these. When you write your paragraph, use one sentence for each of these facts.

3. Look over your list of sensory words and active words. Add any new ones you can come up with.

4. Examine your two topic sentences. Underline the better one.

5. Examine your two concluding sentences. Underline the better one.

6. On the lines below, write a first draft of your descriptive paragraph. *Always keep in mind that you are trying to make the subject come alive to a reader who has never seen it.* (Write the title on the top line.)

_____

_____

_____

_____

_____

_____

_____

_____

_____

_____

_____

_____

© 1995 by John Wiley & Sons, Inc.

Name _____ **Date** _____

Looking Good!
Revising and Writing a Final Copy

DIRECTIONS:

1. Revise your first draft.
   Are your sentences complete and clear?
   Is the spelling correct? Consult a dictionary if necessary.
   Does your topic sentence introduce the subject in an interesting way? Does your concluding sentence sum it up?
   Have you used enough sensory words and active words to make your description vivid?

2. Write your final copy on the lines below. (Place the title on the top line.)

_____

_____

_____

_____

_____

_____

_____

_____

_____

_____

_____

_____

© 1995 by John Wiley & Sons, Inc.

Name _____   **Date** _____

Cut It Out!

There's an old saying, "Too many cooks spoil the broth." That can be applied to writing. Too many words can spoil a paragraph.

Some people think the more words they use, the better the writing. The opposite is true. The only words needed are those that clearly tell what the paragraph is about and add to the vividness and interest. Anything else is clutter, like all the extra stuff crammed into a closet that makes it impossible to find what you're looking for. A cluttered paragraph makes the meaning difficult to discover.

Here is a paragraph that is too wordy:

> The guest room I'm talking about is not just a room that's used for guests. We use it a lot of the time for a lot of different things. Along one wall on one side of the room is my dad's large oak desk with a matching swivel chair in front of it. There's a portable sewing machine in the corner that's seldom used because I don't like to sew and neither does my sister or my mother and father, but my mom sometimes makes hems or sews curtains with it. There's a couch in front of the window that can sometimes be pulled out into a bed when friends, uncles, aunts, or cousins sleep over. The people in my family call this room the spare room.

Here is the same paragraph with some of the excess words cut out:

> The guest room is not just for guests. We use it for a lot of different things. Along one wall is my dad's oak desk with a matching swivel chair. There's a portable sewing machine in the corner that my mom sometimes uses to sew hems or curtains. There's a couch in front of the window that can be pulled out into a bed for friends or relatives who sleep over. We call it the spare room.

DIRECTIONS: Rewrite each sentence on the line below, cutting out unnecessary words.

1. The man that I'm telling you about came to the house we once lived in.

_____

2. All of the students who were in the room at that time were quite still.

_____

3. He was really afraid, you see, that the fierce alien might possibly attack.

_____

4. I actually passed the same test I told you about that I would fail.

_____

© 1995 by John Wiley & Sons, Inc.

Name _____   Date _____

Cut It Out Even More!

Anything that doesn't add to the interest, vividness, or meaning of a paragraph should be taken out. Some words and phrases often used unnecessarily are *really, I'm saying* or *I'm telling you, actually, I guess, along the lines of, quite, the fact that, the reason why, particular, of which, looked like, right away,* and *so.*

Saying the same idea twice using different words is also unnecessary clutter. For example, *If I had a lot of money and could afford it, I would travel* should be *If I had a lot of money, I would travel.* Another example: *He repeated it again* should be *He repeated it.*

DIRECTIONS: Cross out all the unnecessary words and phrases in the following paragraph. Then, rewrite the paragraph on the lines below without the clutter.

> The November day of which I'm speaking about was cold and windy. The weather looked as if it was going to rain. I actually wanted to go shopping, but the reason why I couldn't was because I didn't have a raincoat that I could wear. When I told my mom about the problem I was having with what I wanted to do, she smiled and told me to stay right where I was and not move. She went into another room right away. Then she came out and I saw that she was holding a box in her hands. "Here's your new raincoat," she spoke to me and said. So I was able to go out to the stores shopping after all.

© 1995 by John Wiley & Sons, Inc.

_____

_____

_____

_____

_____

_____

_____

_____

_____

_____

Name _____   **Date** _____

Paragraph Seeds
First Draft

A seed can grow into a flower if it is planted and tended with care. In the same way, the seed of an idea can be developed into a paragraph. In a garden, our tools are spades, pots, fertilizer, and water. The tools of paragraph growing are

1. An interesting topic sentence

2. Three or four sentences that develop the idea in a logical order

3. A concluding sentence that sums up

4. Avoid repetition, remove unnecessary words

5. Sensory words and active verbs that create vivid word pictures

DIRECTIONS: On the lines following each topic sentence below, write the first draft of a paragraph that develops that topic.

1. Some days, it doesn't pay to get up in the morning. _____

_____

_____

_____

_____

_____

2. It was the most unfair thing I had ever seen! _____

_____

_____

_____

_____

_____

© 1995 by John Wiley & Sons, Inc.

© 1995 by John Wiley & Sons, Inc.

Name _____ Date _____

Paragraph Seeds
Revising and Writing a Final Copy

DIRECTIONS: Revise the two paragraphs you wrote for Activity 36A.

1. Is each sentence complete and clear?

2. Are all words spelled correctly? (Check the dictionary.)

3. Is the topic developed in a clear and logical way?

4. Have you used vivid active verbs and sensory words?

5. Have you crossed out any unnecessary words or repetition?

6. Does the concluding paragraph sum up the topic?

Write the final copy of each paragraph on the lines below.

1. _____

_____

_____

_____

_____

_____

_____

2. _____

_____

_____

_____

_____

_____

Name _____   Date _____

Stop That Chop!

It's okay to use a very short sentence in a paragraph. It is not good, however, to write a paragraph that consists only of short sentences. Note the choppiness of the following paragraph:

> Ricky is my best friend. He has shaggy blond hair. His eyes are brown. He is tall. He is skinny. He is good at baseball. He likes soccer. So do I. We have fun together. It's great to have a friend.

If we combine and rearrange some of these sentences and add more vivid description, we would have a paragraph that flows more smoothly, like this:

> Ricky is my best friend. He has brown eyes and shaggy blond hair like a friendly puppy. Some people call him "Beanpole" because he is so tall and skinny. Ricky and I have fun together because we like the same things, such as baseball and soccer. It's great to have a friend!

DIRECTIONS: The sentences in the following paragraph are too short and choppy. Rewrite the paragraph on the lines below. Combine and rearrange some of the sentences and add some vivid descriptions to make the paragraph flow better.

> Wow! What a party I had! It was a surprise. It was my birthday. I came home. The house seemed empty. I looked all around. I wondered where everyone was. Then, I heard a noise. It came from the basement. I went down. The room was dark. Suddenly, the lights went on. Everyone shouted "Happy Birthday!" There were balloons. There was cake and ice cream. I got lots of presents. It was a great birthday surprise. It was the best I ever had.

_____

_____

_____

_____

_____

_____

_____

© 1995 by John Wiley & Sons, Inc.

Name _____   Date _____

Stop That Chop Again!

DIRECTIONS: The following paragraphs are choppy and awkward because the sentences are too short. Rewrite each paragraph on the lines below. Combine and rearrange the sentences and add some vivid language or details that make the narration flow.

   I live on Randolph Street. It is an interesting street. Exciting things happen there. The Foleys live at number 305. That's two houses down from me. Two years ago, Mrs. Foley had five babies. They were quintuplets. Reporters came. So did a TV crew. It was in all the papers. Mr. Bradbury lives in the green house. It's at the end of the block. He's a famous artist. The Trouts raise beagle puppies. They live at number 325. Amy and Sara are my friends. They live next door. That's what Randolph Street is like.

_____

_____

_____

_____

_____

   I had an accident. It was last week. I started a fire. I didn't mean to do it. I was in my room. I had a scented candle. My aunt gave it to me. I got some matches from the kitchen. I brought them to my room. I lit the candle. It smelled nice. I blew out the match. I threw it into the wastebasket. It wasn't out completely. I didn't know that. Then I saw flames. They were coming from the wastebasket. I was scared. I got a pail of water. I threw the water into the wastebasket. I filled up the pail a few times. Finally, the fire went out. I almost set fire to my room. I couldn't believe it!

_____

_____

_____

_____

_____

© 1995 by John Wiley & Sons, Inc.

Name _____ Date _____

Too, Too Much

It's fine to include one or two long sentences in a paragraph. But if most of the sentences are long, it can make the writing unclear and boring as in this paragraph:

My fifth-grade teacher, Mrs. Kasden, was the very, very best teacher that I ever had in all the many years that I've been in the school that I'm going to now. The main reason that she was such a very good teacher was because she cared about each and every kid in the class and was very understanding and was very kind and tried her best to help us with the things with which we had problems. She never screamed and she never said mean things even to some of the students that really deserved to be screamed at sometimes, but she was always patient and always very, very nice. I'm really a lucky kid to have been in the class of a great and wonderful teacher like Mrs. Kasden when I was in fifth grade.

It's easy to make this paragraph more interesting by breaking up the longest sentences. Cutting out unnecessary words and phrases, such as *very, the reason that, each and every, things with which*, and *really* will help. So will taking out things that are repeated. Isn't this better?

My fifth-grade teacher, Mrs. Kasden, was the best teacher I ever had. She was kind and understanding and cared about the kids. When we had problems, she tried to help. Even when students were bad, she never screamed or said mean things but was always patient. I'm lucky to have had a great teacher like Mrs. Kasden.

DIRECTIONS: The following paragraph has too many long sentences. It also has some unnecessary and repetitious words and phrases. Rewrite it more effectively *on a separate sheet of paper.*

My nerdy little brother, Mikey, who is always a real pest, once got lost when our whole family, my mom and dad, my older brother, Luke, and our dear little pet puppy, Wiggles, went for a picnic one Sunday in June to the county park that's real close to our home, only a half-hour away by car. All of the rest of us, not including Mikey, were really busy getting stuff out of the car and getting things set up out on the picnic table. All of a sudden, for some reason, someone noticed that the little nerd, Mikey, was missing, and we all went out all over and searched for him for about twenty minutes or so, and my mom was really starting to get upset, until finally, Mikey just sort of strolled back all by himself and didn't even know why all of the rest of us were really upset. That little nerd, Mikey, can really be a pest, but that was sort of the worst thing he ever did.

© 1995 by John Wiley & Sons, Inc.

Name _____ Date _____

Too, Too Much Again

DIRECTIONS: The following paragraph is difficult to read because the sentences are too long. There are also too many unnecessary words and repetition. Rewrite the paragraph on the lines below. Break up and rearrange the sentences so that they flow better and are easier to understand. Cut out unnecessary words and phrases. Also cut words and phrases that are repeated.

I'll never forget the day I went into the haunted house, even though I really should have known better because I knew it was something that I really shouldn't have done and something that I really didn't have to do. My friends dared me to do it, that's what they did. They were my friends Petey and Patrick, and they dared me to go in, and I did even though everyone in the neighborhood always said that big empty house was haunted. I was in there in that house for ten minutes or so and after that when I came out, Petey and Patrick said that I really looked as if I might actually have seen a ghost in that house. I didn't tell them what happened while I was there inside that house, and I'll never tell anyone about it, not ever, but I can tell you that I'll sure as anything never ever forget that day.

_____

_____

_____

_____

_____

_____

_____

_____

_____

_____

_____

© 1995 by John Wiley & Sons, Inc.

Name _____   **Date** _____

Paragraph Fun
First Draft

DIRECTIONS: The paragraphs below already have a topic sentence. Can you finish them by adding three or four more sentences and a conclusion? Your paragraphs can be either serious or silly, true or imaginary. It's up to you. Write your first drafts on the lines below each topic sentence.

1. Here's what I wish I could see when I look into a mirror. _____

_____

_____

_____

_____

_____

_____

_____

2. Most people want a puppy or kitten as a pet, but not me. _____

_____

_____

_____

_____

_____

_____

© 1995 by John Wiley & Sons, Inc.

Name _____ **Date** _____

Paragraph Fun
Revising and Writing a Final Copy

DIRECTIONS: Revise the two paragraphs you wrote for Activity 39A. Look for the following:

1. Are your sentences clear and complete? Do they vary in size, with some short and some long?

2. Is all spelling correct? (Check in a dictionary.)

3. Have you used vivid language, such as sensory words and active verbs, to make your writing more interesting?

4. Have you cut out unnecessary words and phrases?

5. Have you cut anything that is repeated?

6. Does your concluding sentence sum up the paragraph?

Write your final copy of each paragraph on the lines below.

1. _____

_____

_____

_____

_____

2. _____

_____

_____

_____

_____

© 1995 by John Wiley & Sons, Inc.

Name _____   **Date** _____

More Paragraph Fun
First Draft

DIRECTIONS: The paragraphs below already have a topic sentence. Can you finish them by adding three or four more sentences and a conclusion? Your paragraphs can be either serious or silly, true or imaginary. It's up to you. Write your first drafts on the lines below each topic sentence.

1. I once saw a strange sight on my way to school. _____

_____

_____

_____

_____

_____

_____

_____

2. There's one place I'd rather be than anywhere else in the world. _____

_____

_____

_____

_____

_____

_____

_____

© 1995 by John Wiley & Sons, Inc.

Name _____ **Date** _____

More Paragraph Fun
Revising and Writing a Final Copy

DIRECTIONS: Revise the two paragraphs you wrote for Activity 40A.

1. Are your sentences clear and complete? Are they arranged in logical order?

2. Is your spelling correct? (Check in dictionary?)

3. Have you used vivid language, such as active verbs and sensory words, to make your writing more exciting?

4. Can you add a simile or metaphor to make your paragraph vivid?

5. Are there any unnecessary words or phrases?

6. Have you cut repeated words or phrases?

7. Does your concluding sentence sum up the paragraph?

    Write your final copy of each paragraph on the lines below.

1. _____

_____

_____

_____

_____

_____

2. _____

_____

_____

_____

_____

© 1995 by John Wiley & Sons, Inc.

Name _____ **Date** _____

Shopping List
Prewriting

© 1995 by John Wiley & Sons, Inc.

Paragraph writing can be easy if you think of it as just a list of sentences:

1. The first sentence states the topic.

2. The next three or four sentences support and expand the topic, just as a shopping list supports a shopping trip.

3. The final sentence sums up and concludes the topic.

EXAMPLE:

1. Topic sentence—I wondered what the new market would be like when I went shopping there yesterday.

2. First item on shopping list—fruit

3. Second item on shopping list—chicken

4. Third item on shopping list—ice cream

5. Conclusion—From now on, I plan to do all my shopping at Burton's.

Here's what a paragraph based on this list might look like:

> I wondered what the new market would be like when I went shopping there yesterday. They had a huge selection of fresh, luscious fruit, so I bought three bananas and a pound of red grapes. I was pleased to see that the meat department offered the brand of chicken I prefer. The frozen dessert aisle was such an ice cream lovers paradise that it took a long time to choose among all the brands and flavors. From now on, I plan to do all my shopping at Burton's.

DIRECTIONS: Choose one of the following subjects for a paragraph. Write it on the title line on the next page. Then make a "shopping list" like the one in the example. Next to number 1, list your topic sentence. Under that, continue a numbered list of three or four items that will develop your topic. (Just list the items; don't write sentences yet.) Next to the final number, write your concluding sentence.

Subjects (choose one):   A great book I recently read
An excellent TV show
My favorite meal
My favorite musical group

Write the title you've chosen here: _____

1. _____

2. _____

3. _____

4. _____

5. _____

6. _____

© 1995 by John Wiley & Sons, Inc.

Name _____ **Date** _____

Shopping List
First Draft

DIRECTIONS: Write the first draft of a paragraph. Use the "shopping list" you made for Activity 41A as a guide. Here are some easy steps for you to follow:

1. Copy the title as it appears on your list.

2. Copy the topic sentence as it appears on your list.

3. Write one sentence for each of the supporting items on your list.

4. Copy the concluding sentence as it appears on your list.

(Title) _____

_____

_____

_____

_____

_____

_____

_____

_____

_____

_____

_____

_____

© 1995 by John Wiley & Sons, Inc.

Name _____ **Date** _____

Shopping List
Revising and Writing a Final Copy

DIRECTIONS: Revise the paragraph you wrote for Activity 41B right on that worksheet:

1. Are your sentences clear and complete?

2. Are the sentences arranged in a logical order?

3. Is the topic developed in an interesting manner?

4. Are all words spelled correctly? (Check in a dictionary.)

5. Have you used active verbs and sensory words for vivid and exciting reading?

6. Can you think of one simile or metaphor that would improve the paragraph?

    Are you certain that your paragraph is now as well-written as it can be? Write your final copy on the lines below.

_____

_____

_____

_____

_____

_____

_____

_____

_____

_____

_____

© 1995 by John Wiley & Sons, Inc.

Name _____ **Date** _____

Paragraph Puzzles
First Draft

Here is a paragraph game that is fun, easy, and challenging, all at the same time!

DIRECTIONS: The two paragraphs on this worksheet were once whole. They had an accident. Each paragraph broke apart and lost part of itself. Now they are only fragments. Your job will be to complete each paragraph and make it whole again.

In order to do this, you must carefully read the topic statement and the few sentences that follow. Figure out what the paragraph is about. Then finish each paragraph clearly and logically. You should add at least three or four additional sentences, including a conclusion.

PARAGRAPH PUZZLE #1

My friend Eric is into all kinds of athletics. His favorite sport is baseball because he just happens to be the best hitter our league has had in a million years. He likes biking, too, because _____

_____

_____

_____

_____

PARAGRAPH PUZZLE #2

My mom always complains that I don't eat enough, but there are three kinds of meals I really love. I love the spicy taste of spaghetti and meatballs. At this meal, I often ask for seconds. Chinese food is good, too. _____

_____

_____

_____

_____

_____

© 1995 by John Wiley & Sons, Inc.

Name _____   **Date** _____

Paragraph Puzzles
Revising and Writing a Final Copy

DIRECTIONS: Revise the two paragraphs you completed for Activity 42A. Use the following guidelines (you can change the beginnings, too, if you think they can be improved):

1. Are your sentences clear and complete? Do your subjects and verbs agree?

2. Check in a dictionary if you are not sure of any spelling.

3. Do you use some active verbs and sensory words to make your writing interesting?

4. Do the sentences you wrote add to and complete the subject of the paragraph?

Write your revised paragraphs below.

PARAGRAPH #1

_____

_____

_____

_____

_____

_____

PARAGRAPH #2

_____

_____

_____

_____

_____

_____

© 1995 by John Wiley & Sons, Inc.

Name _____ **Date** _____

Backward Paragraph Puzzles
First Draft

Here are some more paragraph puzzles that are fun to solve.

DIRECTIONS: The two paragraphs on this worksheet have a big problem. They were once whole, but somehow the first half of each paragraph broke off and has been lost. All that's left are the last few sentences. Can you figure out what this paragraph is about from the concluding sentences and those that come before? Make each paragraph complete again by writing a topic sentence at the beginning, followed by two or three additional ones that fit in logically and clearly.

PARAGRAPH PUZZLE #1

_____

_____

_____

_____

_____ I like gym because the games we play are fun, even though I'm not very good at them. Reading hasn't always been my favorite subject, but this year we've read some exciting stories and the teacher tells good jokes. So even though school is boring at times, I really enjoy some of my classes.

PARAGRAPH PUZZLE #2

_____

_____

_____

_____

_____ Betsy's other brother, Jonathan, is only three years old. She likes to help take care of him. Betsy has two sets of grandparents, too. They live nearby and come over a lot. Betsy loves being part of a big, close family.

© 1995 by John Wiley & Sons, Inc.

Name _____ **Date** _____

Backward Paragraph Puzzles
Revising and Writing a Final Copy

DIRECTIONS: Revise the paragraphs you completed in Activity 43A. You may revise the final sentences as well as what you wrote. Use these guidelines:

1. Are your sentences clear and complete?

2. Do your subjects and verbs agree?

3. Use a dictionary to check spelling.

4. Do the sentences you wrote make a logical, complete paragraph that flows easily and makes sense?

Write your revised paragraphs below.

PARAGRAPH #1

_____

_____

_____

_____

_____

_____

PARAGRAPH #2

_____

_____

_____

_____

_____

© 1995 by John Wiley & Sons, Inc.

UNIT THREE

Simple Essays

The essay is often the bugaboo of the writing curriculum. Students sometimes approach it with such dread that one would think they were being asked to produce complex, esoteric scientific or philosophical treatises. At regular intervals there appears some new national survey proving that American students are woefully lacking in essay-writing skills. It has even been suggested that these unfair horrors be completely eliminated and standardized tests be limited to short-answer questions. Thankfully, testmakers have managed so far to avoid such a drastic nonsolution and students must still endure the stress of essay writing.

In most cases, this fear is unnecessary! Basically, essays are little more than expanded paragraphs. A paragraph has a beginning, middle, and end consisting of sentences. An essay has a beginning, middle, and end consisting of paragraphs. Teachers of writing will usually testify that students who have acquired familiarity with paragraph writing and who have then been set to writing essays early and frequently usually have little trouble with this form of communication.

The essay activities in this unit are simple. They are all easy three-paragraph themes. For the most part, they are geared to topics of maximum student interest and can even be fun to do. The steps of the writing process are used for optimum effect. Prewriting activities are particularly stressed in the essay-writing units since structure and clarity of thought are essential for effective essays. In fact, like a mutually-beneficial circle, clear writing needs clear thinking, and the structural requirements of the essay often help the writer to think more clearly.

The activities in this unit are structured in three steps. The first worksheet includes prewriting activities, the second gives explicit directions for writing a first draft, and the third contains instructions for revising and writing a final copy. It is strongly recommended that all three worksheets be used for any of these essay-writing projects.

Name _____   Date _____

I Didn't Know That Was There!
Prewriting

DIRECTIONS: Do you realize that there are objects right under your nose every day that you never even notice—things in your house, your neighborhood, your school? Look around your classroom now. Really look! Chances are you'll be able to point out a few things you've never seen before even though they've been there all along. Perhaps there's a wide pipe in one corner going into a hole in the ceiling . . . or a grating in the floor . . . or an odd-shaped stain on one of the windowshades . . . or a small bookcase in the rear . . . or a welcome sign over the door . . . or . . . well, you get the idea.

You're going to write an essay about these things that you didn't know were there. It's going to be easy to write because you will do it in several steps that will make the final writing simple.

The first step is called *prewriting* or *brainstorming*. It means getting your random thoughts down on paper, and it will help you get ideas. All you have to do is look around the room slowly and carefully. Then, jot down anything you see that you may not have noticed before. Next to the name of each object, write some words that describe it. Next to that, put down any feelings you may have about it, as in the example below:

_____

EXAMPLE: grate in floor—metal, about six inches square, near teacher's desk—I can't believe I never noticed it; what could it be for?

_____

Now, write your list on the lines below. The more objects you can find, the better, but try to list at least three.

_____

_____

_____

_____

_____

_____

_____

_____

© 1995 by John Wiley & Sons, Inc.

Name _____ **Date** _____

I Didn't Know That Was There!
First Draft

DIRECTIONS: Essays are constructed like paragraphs except that they are longer and consist of more than one paragraph.

The easiest essay to write has just three paragraphs. First comes the topic paragraph. This introduces the subject and tries to get the reader's interest. Since you have a whole paragraph to work with, you can use several sentences to introduce your topic in an exciting way. On the lines below, write a draft of your first paragraph. (This is only a first draft, so don't worry about spelling or grammar. Just get it down on paper.)

_____

_____

_____

_____

The second paragraph is the longest. It is the main part of the essay and states all the information you wish to tell about your subject. Since this will be a short, three-paragraph essay, you will not go into much detail. Just state the points you want to make to explain your topic. When you write longer essays, you will need an entire paragraph for each point, but this piece will be short and to the point. Choose three ideas from your brainstorming list and write your second paragraph here.

_____

_____

_____

_____

The third paragraph concludes your essay. Use two or three sentences to restate the topic and to sum up. This is a good place to include your feelings about it.

_____

_____

_____

_____

© 1995 by John Wiley & Sons, Inc.

Name _____   Date _____

I Didn't Know That Was There!
Revising and Writing a Final Copy

DIRECTIONS: Revise your first draft. Make your corrections and changes right on the worksheet. Follow the guidelines below:

1. Is the grammar correct? Do the subjects and verbs agree?

2. Is the spelling correct? Consult the dictionary if you are unsure.

3. Have you used the best word or phrase to convey what you want to say? For example, would *enormous* describe something better than *big*? Would *astonished* describe your feelings better than *surprised*? Would *dull metal* or *gleaming metal* be better than just metal?

4. Did the first paragraph introduce your topic? Can you find a way to make it more exciting? A bit of humor often works well here.

5. In the second paragraph, did you describe your examples in a clear and interesting way? Did you give three examples?

6. In your concluding paragraph, did you restate the topic in a different way? Did you include your own feelings about it?

Now write your revised essay below. Use the back of this paper if you need more room.

I DIDN'T KNOW THAT WAS THERE!

_____

_____

_____

_____

_____

_____

_____

_____

_____

© 1995 by John Wiley & Sons, Inc.

Name _____   **Date** _____

Twenty-First-Century Inventions
Prewriting

DIRECTIONS: Just think of all the marvelous things we now have that weren't around in the nineteenth century—jet planes, space travel, radio, television, computers, dishwashers, videos, compact disks, electronic games, and much more.

Soon, the twenty-first century will arrive. You're going to write about some of the wonders inventors might come up with in the next hundred years. Your ideas might be practical or wild and woolly. They could be things that are possible or fantastic ideas that couldn't really happen. Or could they?

For this prewriting (brainstorming) step, you are going to let your imagination soar. On the lines below, write down whatever ideas come into your head, no matter how ridiculous they might seem. Next to each idea, write a few words to describe this new invention of the future—what it looks like, what it does, and so on.

BRAINSTORMING LIST—TWENTY-FIRST-CENTURY INVENTIONS

_____

_____

_____

_____

_____

_____

_____

_____

_____

_____

_____

© 1995 by John Wiley & Sons, Inc.

Name _____   Date _____

Twenty-First-Century Inventions
First Draft

DIRECTIONS: This is a short, fun-to-write essay. It will have only three paragraphs. The first paragraph should introduce your topic in an interesting way that will be exciting for the reader. Sometimes starting with a question is effective. For example, "What do you think the world of the twenty-first century will be like?" or "What wonders will twenty-first-century inventors bring to our lives?" Can you think of a good question with which to begin your essay? Follow it up with one or two more sentences about this topic. Write a draft of your first paragraph below. (This is only a draft. Don't worry about spelling or grammar. Just get down your ideas.)

_____

_____

_____

_____

   The second paragraph is the main part of your essay. Write a first draft below. Pick out two or three of your best ideas from your brainstorming list. Describe the appearance and function of each one.

_____

_____

_____

_____

   The third and last paragraph will restate the topic in a different way. Try to include some thoughts about the excitement and fun of thinking about the world of the future. Write your draft below.

_____

_____

_____

_____

© 1995 by John Wiley & Sons, Inc.

Name _____ **Date** _____

Twenty-First-Century Inventions
Revising and Writing a Final Copy

DIRECTIONS: Correct and revise your first draft. Try to make it as good as you can. The following guidelines will help:

1. Are your sentences all complete? Do subjects and verbs agree?

2. Check the spelling of difficult words in the dictionary.

3. Did you begin the first paragraph with an exciting question? Is the topic clearly stated?

4. Have you used the most vivid words and phrases to get your ideas across? A simile such as "The Time Traveler looks as simple on the surface as your old family car" can be effective. Try to use one simile in your second paragraph.

5. Does your final paragraph restate the theme and sum up your ideas?

   When you have finished correcting the first draft, write your final copy below. (Use the back of this paper if you need more room.)

TWENTY-FIRST-CENTURY INVENTIONS

_____

_____

_____

_____

_____

_____

_____

_____

_____

_____

© 1995 by John Wiley & Sons, Inc.

Name _____ Date _____

Me, Myself, and I
Prewriting

What do you know more about than anyone else in the world? It's not history or sports or science or math, no matter how smart you may be. The one subject you know better than anyone else is yourself!

The easiest things to write about are familiar subjects. There's no subject as familiar to you as yourself! That's why you're going to be able to do your best writing in this essay.

To make it even easier, your first step will be brainstorming.

DIRECTIONS: On the lines below, write down all the words and phrases you can think of that could be used in a description of yourself. Think about your physical appearance, your family, your friends, your personality, your values, your special interests, your hopes and dreams, things you like and dislike, things you're good at, things that are difficult for you, and so on.

You're not going to use everything on the brainstorming list in your essay, but the more you put down, the more choices you'll have.

BRAINSTORMING LIST—ME, MYSELF, AND I

_____

_____

_____

_____

_____

_____

_____

_____

_____

© 1995 by John Wiley & Sons, Inc.

Name _____   **Date** _____

Me, Myself, and I
First Draft

DIRECTIONS: This is a short, fun-to-write essay. It will have only three paragraphs. The first paragraph should introduce your topic in an exciting way. Capture the reader's attention with the first sentence or sentences. One effective "hook" is the use of humor or surprise. For example, "I have one true, best friend. It's the person I see in the mirror every morning when I brush my teeth." Or "My friends think they really know me. They're in for a big surprise." Or "Help! I have to write a description of the most boring person I know." Well, you get the idea. Write your first paragraph below. Hook your reader with the first sentence. Add two or three more sentences as part of the introduction. (This is a first draft. Don't worry about spelling or grammar.)

_____

_____

_____

The second paragraph is the main part of your essay. Pick out four or five items from your brainstorming list. Write a sentence about each one of these important aspects of you!

_____

_____

_____

_____

_____

_____

The third and final paragraph will restate and sum up the subject. Something amusing could be appropriate here, too. Try to include at least three sentences in this paragraph.

_____

_____

_____

_____

© 1995 by John Wiley & Sons, Inc.

Name _____   Date _____

Me, Myself, and I
Revising and Writing a Final Copy

DIRECTIONS: Correct and revise your first draft. Try to make it as perfect as you can. The following guidelines will help:

1. Are your sentences complete? Do subjects and verbs agree?

2. Check the spelling of difficult words in the dictionary.

3. Did you begin the first paragraph with an interesting, perhaps humorous hook?

4. Have you used active verbs and vivid, sensory words wherever possible?

5. Did you use the final paragraph to sum up this description of yourself in an interesting or amusing way?

When you have finished correcting the first draft, write your final copy below. (Use the back of this paper if you need more room.)

ME, MYSELF, AND I

_____

_____

_____

_____

_____

_____

_____

_____

_____

_____

_____

© 1995 by John Wiley & Sons, Inc.

Name _____ **Date** _____

My Own Special Place
Prewriting

Everyone has at least one place that feels special. It could be a vacation spot you've visited only once or twice or it might be as familiar and ordinary as the comfy couch you sprawl on to read or watch TV.

Think about this place. Try to bring to mind as many details as you can about the spot and all its surroundings. Then, give some thought to how this place makes you feel and why it makes you feel that way.

DIRECTIONS: This brainstorming list will be divided into two sections. The first section will include all the words and phrases you can think of that describe what your special place looks like. The second section of the brainstorming list will include all the words and phrases you can come up with that describe your feelings about this place and why you feel that way.

BRAINSTORMING LIST—MY OWN SPECIAL PLACE

PART ONE—WHAT THIS PLACE LOOKS LIKE: _____

_____

_____

_____

_____

_____

PART TWO—HOW THIS PLACE MAKES ME FEEL: _____

_____

_____

_____

_____

_____

© 1995 by John Wiley & Sons, Inc.

Name _____   **Date** _____

My Own Special Place
First Draft

DIRECTIONS: One way of grabbing interest in the first paragraph is to use a hint of mystery in the introduction. Here are some examples of how this might be done in the first paragraph of this essay. (1) "There is a place you can never find. I will never tell a living soul where it is. It is my own special spot." (2) "Can you guess where my own special place is? It is a spot that is familiar to everybody in this class. I wonder how many of you will recognize it." Can you include a bit of mystery in your introduction? Write your first paragraph below. (This is only a draft, so don't worry about spelling or grammar.)

_____

_____

_____

_____

© 1995 by John Wiley & Sons, Inc.

The second paragraph is the main part of your essay. Choose the most vivid words and phrases from your brainstorming list and write three or four descriptive sentences. Then add one or two additional sentences to show your feelings about this place.

_____

_____

_____

_____

_____

In the third and last paragraph, restate briefly in a different way that this is your own special place and how you feel about it. If you included some mystery in the introduction, use it in the conclusion too, such as, "Have you guessed where this place is?" Write your draft below.

_____

_____

_____

_____

Name _____   Date _____

My Own Special Place
Revising and Writing a Final Copy

DIRECTIONS: Correct and revise your first draft. The following guidelines will help:

1. Are your sentences all complete? Do subjects and verbs agree?

2. Check the spelling of difficult words in the dictionary.

3. Did you begin the first paragraph interestingly, perhaps with a hint of mystery?

4. Did you use vivid, sensory words to make your description come alive to the reader? Try to add at least one more sensory word.

5. When you describe your feelings about this place, try to use at least one simile to get your ideas across to the reader.

6. Does your final paragraph sum up and complete the essay?

When you have finished correcting the first draft, write your final copy below. Indent at the beginning of each paragraph. (Use the back of this paper if you need more room.)

MY OWN SPECIAL PLACE

_____

_____

_____

_____

_____

_____

_____

_____

_____

© 1995 by John Wiley & Sons, Inc.

Name _____   **Date** _____

My Hero
Prewriting

Is there someone you admire? Perhaps you look up to a famous leader such as a president or mayor or general, living or historical. It could be a sports figure you wish you could be like, or a film star or pop music singer. Your hero or heroine might not be well-known at all, but an ordinary person—someone in your family or neighborhood or school. Is it possible that you most admire someone who isn't even real—a character from a book or movie or TV show?

DIRECTIONS: On the lines below, write down all the words and phrases you can think of that describe the hero or heroine you have chosen. Think about what he or she looks like. List words and phrases that describe his character and personality, where the person comes from, and what kind of life he or she lives. Most of all, be sure to list the aspects of appearance, character, personality, and achievements that are most admirable.

BRAINSTORMING LIST—MY HERO

_____

_____

_____

_____

_____

_____

_____

_____

_____

_____

_____

_____

_____

© 1995 by John Wiley & Sons, Inc.

© 1995 by John Wiley & Sons, Inc.

Name _____   Date _____

My Hero
First Draft

DIRECTIONS: This is a short, easy-to-write essay with only three paragraphs. The first paragraph should introduce your topic. You can start with an ordinary sentence such as, "One person I admire a lot is Abraham Lincoln." Or you might think up something creative and attention-catching like, "What would have happened to our country if it did not have a leader like Abraham Lincoln during its darkest hour?" Follow up the first sentence with two or three more that identify the subject to your reader. You can state the person's name right away, but it could also be effective to lead up to it with the first few sentences and then tell who the person is in the last sentence.

Write your first paragraph below. It should have at least three sentences. (This is a first draft. Don't worry about spelling or grammar.)

_____

_____

_____

_____

The second paragraph is the main part of your essay. Choose four or five items from your brainstorming list that describe your hero and tell why you admire him or her. Write a sentence about each one.

_____

_____

_____

_____

The third and final paragraph will restate the identity of your hero or heroine and sum up what you admire about him or her. There should be at least three sentences in the final paragraph.

_____

_____

_____

_____

Name _____   **Date** _____

My Hero
Revising and Writing a Final Copy

DIRECTIONS: Correct and revise your first draft. Try to make it as perfect as you can. The following guidelines will help:

1. Are your sentences clear and complete? Do subjects and verbs agree?

2. Does your first paragraph identify your subject in an interesting way?

3. Check the spelling of difficult words in the dictionary.

4. Have you used active verbs and vivid, sensory words and phrases wherever possible?

5. Does the final paragraph restate the name of your subject and sum up the meaning of the essay?

Write the final copy of your essay below. Be sure to indent at the beginning of each paragraph. (Use the back of this paper if you need more room.)

MY HERO

_____

_____

_____

_____

_____

_____

_____

_____

_____

_____

_____

_____

© 1995 by John Wiley & Sons, Inc.

Name _____   Date _____

The Yummiest Meal of All
Prewriting

There is one topic that interests almost everyone—food! It's fun to compare our likes and dislikes. What's truly amazing is how people have such different tastes. One person may put ketchup on a hot dog. Another thinks that anything but mustard on hot dogs is totally disgusting.

You're going to be positive here and think about wonderful foods—in fact, a whole meal that makes you feel like running to the dinner table. Then you are going to write a mouth-watering description of an ideal meal.

DIRECTIONS: In the first column below, write down the names of all the foods that you love to eat. Don't decide yet which ones you're going to include in your ideal meal. Just list everything you like to eat. That way you'll have plenty to choose from when you finally write your essay.

In the second column, list as many adjectives and descriptive phrases you can think of that apply to food. You should be able to come up with lots of sensory words and phrases.

BRAINSTORMING LIST—THE YUMMIEST MEAL OF ALL

LIST OF FOODS   *LIST OF DESCRIPTIVE WORDS*

© 1995 by John Wiley & Sons, Inc.

Name _____ **Date** _____

The Yummiest Meal of All
First Draft

DIRECTIONS: This simple essay should be as easy to write as talking to friends about a scrumptious meal. There will be only three paragraphs.

The first paragraph will introduce your topic. Use the first sentence to tell readers what the essay is about and catch their interest. You could use an amusing beginning such as, "My family thinks I'm a weird eater." Or start with a question, "Are your tastes in food ordinary or strange?" Follow up with two or three more sentences that state and describe your topic as the tastiest meal in the world.

Write your first paragraph below. It should have at least three sentences. (This is a first draft. Don't worry about spelling or grammar.)

_____

_____

_____

_____

The second paragraph is the main part of your essay. Choose three or four foods from your list. You might have an appetizer, a main dish, and a dessert, but you can pick any foods you wish. Write one sentence about each of these foods. Use plenty of mouth-watering sensory words.

_____

_____

_____

_____

The third and final paragraph should restate and sum up the subject. There should be at least three sentences in the final paragraph.

_____

_____

_____

_____

© 1995 by John Wiley & Sons, Inc.

Name _____ **Date** _____

The Yummiest Meal of All
Revising and Writing a Final Copy

DIRECTIONS: Correct and revise your first draft.

1. Are your sentences clear and complete? Do subjects and verbs agree?

2. Does your first paragraph identify the topic in an interesting way, perhaps with a question or an amusing first sentence?

3. Check the spelling of difficult words in the dictionary.

4. Have you used sensory words and phrases (especially taste and smell words) to describe your foods?

5. Does the final paragraph restate and sum up the topic?

Write the final copy of your essay below. Indent at the beginning of each paragraph. (Use the back of this paper if you need more room.)

THE YUMMIEST MEAL OF ALL

_____

_____

_____

_____

_____

_____

_____

_____

_____

_____

_____

© 1995 by John Wiley & Sons, Inc.

Name _____   **Date** _____

One Hour in a Supermarket
Prewriting

Some people love to shop till they drop. Others think that shopping is the pits. Where do you stand?

In this activity, you are going to describe one hour in a supermarket. The incidents you write about can be true or imaginary. Before you start, you are going to make a list of the things you might see in a supermarket, such as the foods, the different sections and aisles, and the people (shoppers and workers). Include in your list incidents that might be happening, such as a screaming baby trying to climb out of a cart or a customer at the checkout complaining about a wrong price.

DIRECTIONS: In the first column of your brainstorming list, write down what objects and people you might see in a supermarket. In the second column, list at least four or five incidents that might happen there.

© 1995 by John Wiley & Sons, Inc.

BRAINSTORMING LIST—ONE HOUR IN A SUPERMARKET

OBJECTS AND PEOPLE	*INCIDENTS*
_____	_____
_____	_____
_____	_____
_____	_____
_____	_____
_____	_____
_____	_____
_____	_____

Name _____ **Date** _____

One Hour in a Supermarket
First Draft

DIRECTIONS: It will be fun to imagine one hour in a supermarket. You can write about things you've really seen happen or use your imagination. Your description can be serious or funny. Your brainstorming list will be a big help. The first paragraph should introduce your topic and catch the readers' interest, such as, "In a supermarket, one hour can seem like a hundred." Or "I'll never forget that hour in the supermarket!"

Write your first paragraph below. It should have at least three sentences. (This is only a first draft, so don't worry about spelling or grammar. Just concentrate on getting down your thoughts.)

_____

_____

_____

_____

The second paragraph is the main part of your essay. Use items from the second column of your brainstorming list to tell what happened. Use items from the first column of your brainstorming list to describe the background, such as, "In the fruit section, a baby was screaming and trying to climb out of the cart. The baby was reaching for a ripe, yellow banana." This paragraph should contain at least four or five sentences.

_____

_____

_____

_____

In the third paragraph, restate and sum up the topic. You might also want to include your own feelings about supermarkets here.

_____

_____

_____

_____

© 1995 by John Wiley & Sons, Inc.

Name _____   Date _____

One Hour in a Supermarket
Revising and Writing a Final Copy

DIRECTIONS: Correct and revise your first draft.

1. Are your sentences complete? Do subjects and verbs agree?

2. Does your first paragraph introduce the subject interestingly?

3. Use a dictionary to check spelling.

4. Have you used active verbs and vivid, sensory words and phrases wherever possible?

5. Are the incidents you've chosen the best and most interesting?

6. Does the final paragraph restate and sum up the topic?

Write the final copy of your essay below. Indent at the beginning of each paragraph. (Use the back of this paper if you need more room.)

ONE HOUR IN A SUPERMARKET

_____

_____

_____

_____

_____

_____

_____

_____

_____

_____

_____

© 1995 by John Wiley & Sons, Inc.

© 1995 by John Wiley & Sons, Inc.

Name _____   **Date** _____

A Look at Me, Ten Years From Now
Prewriting

How would you like to be 10 years older than you are right now? What do you imagine or hope you will look like then? What do you think will be going on in your life? Where will you be living? Where will you be going to school? Who will be your friends? What will you be able to do then that you can't do now? Is there anything you think you will miss about your present age?

In this activity, you are going to look into an imaginary crystal ball and see yourself as you will be 10 years from now. It will help to make a brainstorming list first.

DIRECTIONS: On the lines below, write down all the words and phrases you can think of that might describe you and your life 10 years from now. These can be descriptions of your appearance, your lifestyle, your hobbies, your jobs, your activities, and your accomplishments.

BRAINSTORMING LIST—A LOOK AT ME, TEN YEARS FROM NOW

_____

_____

_____

_____

_____

_____

_____

_____

_____

_____

_____

_____

_____

Name _____   **Date** _____

A Look at Me, Ten Years From Now
First Draft

DIRECTIONS: Are you ready to look into your crystal ball and see yourself 10 years from now? The first paragraph of this short, easy essay should introduce your topic. You can use a serious, factual beginning, such as, "Ten years from now, I'll be a very different person from who I am now." Or a question, "Is it possible to see 10 years into the future?" Or something amusing, "I may be a nerd now, but wait until you see me in 10 years!"

Write your first paragraph below. It should have at least three sentences. (This is a first draft, so don't worry about accuracy. Just get down your thoughts.)

_____

_____

_____

_____

The second paragraph is the main part of your essay. Choose four or five items from your brainstorming list. Write one sentence about each. You can choose to be serious or funny or a combination of both.

_____

_____

_____

_____

_____

In your third and final paragraph, restate and sum up your topic. Include here how you feel about these possibilities for the future.

_____

_____

_____

_____

© 1995 by John Wiley & Sons, Inc.

© 1995 by John Wiley & Sons, Inc.

Name _____   **Date** _____

A Look at Me, Ten Years From Now
Revising and Writing a Final Copy

DIRECTIONS: Correct and revise your first draft.

1. Are your sentences clear and complete? Do subjects and verbs agree?

2. Does your first paragraph introduce the topic interestingly?

3. Use a dictionary to check spelling.

4. Have you used active verbs and vivid, sensory words and phrases?

5. Does the final paragraph sum up the topic and your feelings about it?

Write the final copy of your essay below. Indent at the beginning of each paragraph. (Use the back of this paper if you need more room.)

A LOOK AT ME, TEN YEARS FROM NOW

_____

_____

_____

_____

_____

_____

_____

_____

_____

_____

_____

_____

_____

Name _____ **Date** _____

My Neighborhood
Prewriting

The easiest things to write about are those that you know best. What could be more familiar to you than the neighborhood in which you live? There are many things about your neighborhood that would interest others—the houses on your block, the people who live in them, their gardens and trees, the cars and trucks that come down your street, stores and other buildings nearby, parks and playgrounds, and so on. A list of all these details will help you organize and write your essay.

DIRECTIONS: On the lines below, write down all the words and phrases you can think of that describe your neighborhood. It might be helpful to arrange your list in three columns.

In the first column, list words and phrases that apply to the appearance of your neighborhood—buildings, streets, gardens, stores, and so on.

In the second column, list words and phrases about the people (and animals?) in your neighborhood.

In the third column, list words and phrases about life in your neighborhood—parties, friendships, special events, and so on.

© 1995 by John Wiley & Sons, Inc.

BRAINSTORMING LIST—MY NEIGHBORHOOD

BUILDINGS, AND SO ON	*PEOPLE*	*EVENTS*

Name _____   **Date** _____

My Neighborhood
First Draft

DIRECTIONS: It's easy to write a simple essay about your neighborhood with the help of your brainstorming list. The first paragraph should introduce the topic in an interesting way. Here are some beginnings other students have used: "I could walk through my neighborhood blindfolded." "I would hate to live anywhere else but in my neighborhood." "Do you think your neighborhood is weird? Wait till you hear about mine!"

Write your first paragraph below. It should have at least three sentences. (This is a first draft, so don't worry about grammar or spelling. Just get down your thoughts.)

_____

_____

_____

_____

The second paragraph is the main part of your essay. Choose several items from each column of your brainstorming list. Write one sentence about each. The first couple of sentences can be about the appearance of your neighborhood Write two sentences about the people. Use the last sentence or two to tell what goes on there.

_____

_____

_____

_____

In your third paragraph, restate and sum up your topic. This would be a good place to include your own feelings about your neighborhood.

_____

_____

_____

_____

© 1995 by John Wiley & Sons, Inc.

Name _____ Date _____

My Neighborhood
Revising and Writing a Final Copy

DIRECTIONS: Correct and revise your first draft.

1. Are your sentences complete? Do subjects and verbs agree?

2. Do you introduce the topic in an interesting way?

3. Use a dictionary to check spelling.

4. Are your thoughts arranged in a clear and logical order?

5. Does your final paragraph sum up the topic?

    Write the final copy of your essay below. Indent at the beginning of each paragraph. (Use the back of this paper if you need more room.)

MY NEIGHBORHOOD

_____

_____

_____

_____

_____

_____

_____

_____

_____

_____

_____

© 1995 by John Wiley & Sons, Inc.

Name _____   **Date** _____

One Great Day!
Prewriting

Was there one day during the past year that stands out in your memory? Was there a really special day? It might have been a holiday like Thanksgiving or Halloween, your birthday, a memorable trip, a family celebration, or a special event that meant a lot to you.

Maybe you've had more than one such wonderful day. Lucky you! But for this essay, you are going to choose just one to write about—one great day! A good brainstorming list will help you get down and organize your ideas. It should also provide you with most of the words and phrases you will need to describe this one great day!

DIRECTIONS: On the lines below, write down the special day you have chosen to write about. Follow that with all the words and phrases that come into your mind about that day. Words and phrases about the surroundings, weather, people, objects, and events would be appropriate. Hint: When you think your list is complete, don't stop. Add some more. Sometimes the ideas that come last turn out to be the best.

BRAINSTORMING LIST—ONE GREAT DAY!

_____

_____

_____

_____

_____

_____

_____

_____

_____

_____

_____

© 1995 by John Wiley & Sons, Inc.

Name _____ **Date** _____

One Great Day!
First Draft

DIRECTIONS: It should be easy for you to describe your special day with your brainstorming list in front of you. The first paragraph introduces your topic. Here are some sample first sentences other students have used: "I'll never forget that day!" "There'll never be another day like that!" "Last Christmas, my whole life changed." Follow your first sentence with two or three more to expand your introduction.

Write your first paragraph below. It should have at least three sentences. (This is a first draft, so don't worry about accuracy. Just get down your thoughts.)

_____

_____

_____

_____

The second paragraph is the main part of your essay. Tell about your great day. Describe what happened, where, who was there, and how it made you feel. This paragraph should have at least four sentences.

_____

_____

_____

Your third and final paragraph will restate and sum up your topic. This would also be a good place to explain why this day was so important.

_____

_____

_____

_____

© 1995 by John Wiley & Sons, Inc.

Name _____ **Date** _____

One Great Day!
Revising and Writing a Final Copy

DIRECTIONS: Correct and revise your first draft.

1. Are your sentences complete? Do subjects and verbs agree?

2. Use a dictionary to check spelling.

3. Does your first paragraph introduce the topic in an interesting way?

4. Does your second paragraph describe the event in a clear and logical manner?

5. Does the final paragraph restate the topic and sum up the importance of this day?

Write the final copy of your essay below. Indent at the beginning of each paragraph. (Use the back of this paper if you need more room.)

ONE GREAT DAY!

_____

_____

_____

_____

_____

_____

_____

_____

_____

_____

_____

_____

_____

© 1995 by John Wiley & Sons, Inc.

Name _____   Date _____

Home Sweet Home
Prewriting

Have you ever read a description of a house that seemed familiar to you even though you had never been there? Even a short description can make a place come alive, as in this example:

> "There was a "For Sale" sign on the house. It was a great, rambling three-story building covered with layers of thick green ivy. There were paths and gardens in back and all around were acres of soft, deep woods. Stately white columns guarded the front entrance. Inside were many interesting nooks and crannies and a large spooky attic."

Here are some of the words and phrases that make this description so vivid: *great; rambling; thick green ivy; soft, deep woods; stately; guarded*; and *large spooky attic*.

Places that seem ordinary can be made interesting through the use of sensory language (*soft, deep woods*) and active verbs (*guarded*).

What could be a more ordinary and everyday sort of place than your own home? You take it for granted—it's where you live. But could you describe it to someone who has never seen it? Using sensory language and active verbs will help make your description more vivid.

DIRECTIONS: On the lines below, prepare a brainstorming list of words and phrases that could be used to describe your house or apartment. (Examples: faded red brick, small and cozy, sunlit kitchen, gleaming white-tiled bathroom, toy-cluttered room, and so on.) Think about how the building looks from the outside and then go through every room in your mind. You're going to want many more words on your brainstorming list than you're actually going to use in your essay. The longer your list, the more choices you'll have to use the very best words for your essay.

BRAINSTORMING LIST—HOME SWEET HOME

_____

_____

_____

_____

_____

_____

© 1995 by John Wiley & Sons, Inc.

Name _____   **Date** _____

Home Sweet Home
First Draft

DIRECTIONS: It's easy to write a description of a place you know as well as your own home, especially if the description consists of just three paragraphs. Use lots of sensory words and active verbs to make your readers see it the way you do. Your brainstorming list should be a big help.

Introduce the subject in your first paragraph. Your topic sentence can be the first sentence in that paragraph or the last. The introduction can be appealing (There's one place I love better than any spot on Earth.") or funny ("What a dump!"). Remember—this is just a first draft.

Write your first paragraph on the lines below.

_____

_____

_____

_____

In the second paragraph, describe the outside of the building, the arrangement of the rooms, their general appearance, and some interesting, vivid details. This paragraph should have at least four sentences.

_____

_____

_____

_____

Your third and final paragraph will restate and sum up your topic. This would be a good place to include your own feelings about this home. Include at least three sentences in your final paragraph.

_____

_____

_____

_____

© 1995 by John Wiley & Sons, Inc.

Name _____   Date _____

Home Sweet Home
Revising and Writing a Final Copy

DIRECTIONS: Correct and revise your first draft.

1. Does your first paragraph introduce the topic interestingly?

2. Does your second paragraph give a clear and vivid description of your home? Have you used lively sensory language? Look at your brainstorming list again. Have you left out anything that might make your description even better?

3. Does the final paragraph restate the topic and give some of your own feelings about it?

4. Are your sentences complete? Do subjects and verbs agree?

5. Use a dictionary to check spelling.

    Write the final copy of your essay below. Indent at the beginning of each paragraph. (Use the back of this paper if you need more room.)

HOME SWEET HOME

© 1995 by John Wiley & Sons, Inc.

_____

_____

_____

_____

_____

_____

_____

_____

_____

_____

Name _____ **Date** _____

The Ideal Parent
Prewriting

Here's a chance for you to use your imagination in an essay. What if kids could choose their own parents? Wow! Wouldn't that be something? What kind of mom would you pick? What sort of dad? What jobs would they have? Would you prefer a stay-at-home mom or a working mom? How about a stay-at-home dad? What would they look like? What kind of personalities would they have? What would they like to do? What rules would they have? How would they treat you and your brothers or sisters? What things would the family do together?

A good brainstorming list will help you sort out your ideas and make it much easier to write an essay.

DIRECTIONS: This brainstorming list is divided into three parts. In the first section, write down all the words and phrases you can think of to describe an ideal mom. In the second section, write down words and phrases about an ideal dad. In the last section, write words and phrases that describe how they would be and what they would do as parents together.

BRAINSTORMING LIST—THE IDEAL PARENT

THE IDEAL MOM: _____

_____

_____

_____

THE IDEAL DAD: _____

_____

_____

_____

THE IDEAL PARENTS: _____

_____

_____

_____

© 1995 by John Wiley & Sons, Inc.

Name _____ **Date** _____

The Ideal Parent
First Draft

DIRECTIONS: It should be easy to describe ideal parents using your brainstorming list. In the first paragraph, introduce the topic interestingly. (Example: "Kids are stuck with their parents, just as our parents are stuck with us. What if it was different? What if kids could choose the sort of parents they want? What kind of mom and dad would you pick?")

Write your own first paragraph below. It should have at least three sentences. (This is a first draft, so don't worry about accuracy. Just get down your ideas.)

_____

_____

_____

_____

The second paragraph is the main part of the essay. Here's one way to organize it. First, describe the ideal mom. Then, describe the ideal dad. Last, describe the ideal parents together. Your brainstorming list will come in handy. This paragraph should have at least four sentences.

_____

_____

_____

_____

Sum up your ideas about perfect parents in the third paragraph. This would be a good place to include some thoughts about whether or not it would be a good idea for kids to have this choice.

_____

_____

_____

_____

© 1995 by John Wiley & Sons, Inc.

Name _____ **Date** _____

The Ideal Parent
Revising and Writing a Final Copy

DIRECTIONS: Correct and revise your first draft.

1. Does your first paragraph introduce the topic interestingly?

2. Does your second paragraph clearly describe the ideal mom, the ideal dad, and the ideal parents?

3. Does the last paragraph restate and sum up the topic and your thoughts about it?

4. Are your sentences complete? Do subjects and verbs agree?

5. Check the spelling of difficult words in a dictionary.

    Write the final copy of your essay below. Indent at the beginning of each paragraph. (Use the back of this paper if you need more room.)

THE IDEAL PARENT

_____

_____

_____

_____

_____

_____

_____

_____

_____

_____

_____

_____

© 1995 by John Wiley & Sons, Inc.

Name _____   Date _____

Easy as Pie
Prewriting

Has it ever amazed you to discover that a task you had to sweat over turned out to be as "easy as pie" for someone else? You've probably also noticed just the opposite—something that comes to you quite easily seems to be difficult for other kids.

We all have our own special talents as well as our own particular weaknesses. In this essay, you're going to concentrate on something positive and fun—the things that you are good at. Chances are there are a lot more things that come fairly easily to you than you think.

A brainstorming list will help you come up with your special talents as well as examples of how they've come in handy.

DIRECTIONS: This brainstorming list is divided into two columns. In the first column, list those things that come easily to you. In the second column, list specific instances where these talents have been helpful. (For example, a talent in math may have helped you notice an overcharge your mom was about to pay in a store; perhaps your baseball skills helped your team win an important game; your ability to cook may have made it possible to surprise your parents with a great anniversary dinner; your talent for memorization helps you get good grades at school, and so on.)

© 1995 by John Wiley & Sons, Inc.

BRAINSTORMING LIST—EASY AS PIE

TALENTS	*EXAMPLES*
_____	_____
_____	_____
_____	_____
_____	_____
_____	_____
_____	_____
_____	_____
_____	_____

Name _____ **Date** _____

Easy as Pie
First Draft

© 1995 by John Wiley & Sons, Inc.

DIRECTIONS: This essay will be easy if you use your brainstorming list. In your first paragraph, introduce the topic in a way that will be interesting to the reader. Starting with a question can be a good "hook," as in this example: "Do you ever feel that you just can't do anything right? It's happened to me often. At those times, it's hard to remember that there are things I'm good at—things that are as easy as pie for me."

Write your first paragraph here. It should have at least three sentences. Use a question as a "hook." This is just a first draft.

_____

_____

_____

_____

The second paragraph is the main part of the essay. From your brainstorming list, choose two or three of the things that are easy for you. Mention each one, followed by a short description of one way this skill has been helpful. This paragraph will have at least four sentences.

_____

_____

_____

_____

_____

In the third paragraph, restate and sum up the topic.

_____

_____

_____

_____

109

Easy as Pie
Revising and Writing a Final Copy

DIRECTIONS: Correct and revise your first draft.

1. Does your first paragraph introduce the topic? Have you used an interesting "hook," such as a question?

2. Do you describe several of your "easy as pie" skills? Is each one followed by a concrete example of how it is useful?

3. Does the final paragraph restate and sum up the topic?

4. Are your sentences complete? Do subjects and verbs agree?

5. Use a dictionary to check spelling.

Write the final copy of your essay below. Indent at the beginning of each paragraph. (Use the back of this paper if you need more room.)

EASY AS PIE

_____

_____

_____

_____

_____

_____

_____

_____

_____

_____

© 1995 by John Wiley & Sons, Inc.

Name _____ Date _____

Boy, Is This Hard!
Prewriting

We all face challenges in life when we have to do something difficult. But what's hard for one person can be easy for someone else. Everybody has different talents. A genius in school may be uncoordinated at sports. A great athlete might have trouble with reading. Perhaps you're terrific at working with engines and other mechanical stuff but quiet and uncomfortable with groups of people. It's good to be aware of your strengths and weaknesses. That way you'll know that you have to work harder to succeed in tasks that don't come easily.

In this essay, you are going to discuss those things that are hard for you and how that affects your life. A brainstorming list will help you get ready.

DIRECTIONS: This brainstorming list is divided into two columns. In the first column, list those things that are hard for you to do. In the second column, list specific instances where these weaknesses have affected you in either good or bad ways. (For example, maybe you had to study for hours to get a good grade in reading; your best buddy had to practice with you every afternoon for weeks so that you could make the soccer team; maybe being shy kept you from becoming friends with someone you really liked, and so on.)

© 1995 by John Wiley & Sons, Inc.

BRAINSTORMING LIST—BOY, IS THIS HARD!

DIFFICULT THINGS	*EXAMPLES*
_____	_____
_____	_____
_____	_____
_____	_____
_____	_____
_____	_____
_____	_____

Name _____   **Date** _____

Boy, Is This Hard!
First Draft

DIRECTIONS: Your first paragraph will state the topic. One way to do this in a lively fashion is to begin with a humorous statement, as in this example: "Did you think I was perfect? Sure you did! But, do you know what? I'm not! That's right. There are some things that even I have trouble with!"

Write your first paragraph here. It should have at least three sentences. Can you include some humor? (This is just a first draft.)

_____

_____

_____

_____

The second paragraph is the main part of the essay. From your brainstorming list, choose two or three of the things that are hard for you. State each one, followed by a short description of how this has affected you. This paragraph will have at least four sentences.

_____

_____

_____

_____

_____

In the third paragraph, restate and sum up the topic.

_____

_____

_____

_____

© 1995 by John Wiley & Sons, Inc.

Name _____   **Date** _____

Boy, Is This Hard!
Revising and Writing a Final Copy

DIRECTIONS: Correct and revise your first draft.

1. Does your first paragraph introduce the topic in a lively way?

2. Does your second paragraph list several activities that are difficult for you? Is each statement followed by an example of how it has affected your life?

3. Does the last paragraph restate and sum up the topic?

4. Are your sentences complete? Do subjects and verbs agree?

5. Check spelling in a dictionary.

Write the final copy of your essay below. Indent at the beginning of each paragraph. (Use the back of this paper if you need more room.)

BOY, IS THIS HARD!

_____

_____

_____

_____

_____

_____

_____

_____

_____

_____

_____

_____

© 1995 by John Wiley & Sons, Inc.

UNIT FOUR

More Complex Essays

Too many youngsters never really master the art of essay writing. These are the same people who, as adults, have difficulty with the writing skills that are a necessary aspect of much business and professional life. One indication of the depth of this problem is the burgeoning army of writing professionals who are invited by companies and business organizations to offer workshops and seminars to their employees. Why is this necessary? Why do so many otherwise capable and efficient workers produce written work that is rambling, confused, and often incoherent?

Most students today do receive writing instruction. Sometimes, however, there is so much concentration on encouraging these boys and girls to overcome strong writing blocks that there may be too much emphasis on freedom, creativity, and unrestricted self-expression. Not that there is anything wrong with these methods. Far from it! Young people need to learn that writing can be easy, fun, and fulfilling. But one goal does not have to exclude another. In addition to imaginative and expressive writing, students can also learn the discipline and structure that makes for competent exposition.

It is also important for these youngsters to have many successful experiences with this type of writing. They need to do it over and over again as much as possible for these techniques to become thoroughly ingrained as a lifelong skill. The activities in this unit are designed to guide students step by step in the form and structure of essay writing and clear exposition, and to provide the supplementary practice necessary to develop competence in this form of writing. These include prewriting activities (research, brainstorming, lists, and outlines), writing a first draft (with guidelines for organizing and paragraphing), and revising and writing a final copy.

Younger students or older ones who have difficulty with these essays are strongly advised to first acquire familiarity with the simple three-paragraph essays in Unit Three. Mastery of these easy-to-do themes should prepare students to progress naturally and without too much effort into the more complex ones in this chapter.

Name _____ Date _____

Great Friends
Prewriting

DIRECTIONS: What makes a good friend or even a great friend? You probably have your own ideas about the qualities you look for in a friend.

Before you shape these ideas into an essay, it helps to jot down all your thoughts on this subject. This is called *brainstorming*. It is an important first step in helping to transfer ideas from your brain to paper. It can be fun and eye-opening for a group of people to brainstorm together, but it's also effective to do it yourself.

On the lines below, write all the words and phrases that come into your head about friendship. It might be helpful to put down the names of several good friends you have known. Next to each name, write down what these people were like and list the qualities that you liked best about each. Your list might look like this:

Timmy—a fun guy, clowns around a lot, always cheerful, laughs at my jokes, tells good jokes, never says anything bad about others, and likes baseball.

Pat—lives next door, has a nice mom and dad, has lots of great toys and games, always willing to share, gave me a new bat and ball for my birthday, fun for overnights at his house or mine, and smiles a lot.

Ethan—smart, helps me with math, is never grouchy, and is on my Little League team.

Now, make your own list below. List as many kids as you can, but try to have at least three:

_____

_____

_____

_____

_____

_____

_____

_____

_____

_____

© 1995 by John Wiley & Sons, Inc.

Name _____   **Date** _____

Great Friends
First Draft

DIRECTIONS: Look at the list for the example in Activity 58A. If you study it carefully, you'll notice that the three great friends have several things in common. They seem to be fun to be with, they are cheerful, and they all like baseball. Obviously, the writer likes these qualities in a friend. Some of them are great for special reasons, such as having a house where it's fun to sleep over or being smart.

Now look at the list you made. At the bottom, write down the qualities all your good friends have in common. Then list some individual qualities that seem important to you. Now you are ready to write a first draft of your essay about great friends. Here's how to set it up:

In the first paragraph, state the topic and then briefly list the three or four things that are most important in a friend. This is a first draft, so don't worry about spelling or grammar. Just try to get your thoughts onto the paper. Use a separate sheet of paper. Your first paragraph might look something like this:

> I have great friends! When I think about the kids who mean the most to me, I realize that there are some things they have in common. They are usually cheerful. They are great fun to be with. They all share my love of baseball.

Next, write a paragraph about each of the items mentioned in your first paragraph. (This adds up to three paragraphs.) Each paragraph should have its own topic sentence, as in the example below:

> My great friends are cheerful most of the time. I don't really like to be with grouchy people. I only remember my best friend, Timmy, being grumpy once. That was when his kid sister hammered his computer to pieces. Even then, he got over it quickly. All my great friends laugh and smile a lot.
>
> I like to have a good time and I like people who know how to do that. Timmy is always coming up with these great jokes. I laugh all the time when I'm with him. Pat has a great sense of humor, too, and so does Ethan.
>
> Baseball is really important to me. Pat and Ethan are baseball nuts, too. They're both on my Little League team. We all spend a lot of our free time practicing out on the ball field or in our backyards.

Finally, finish your first draft with a concluding paragraph, like this one:

> I like friends who are like me—cheerful, fun to be with, and crazy for baseball. Other people may look for different qualities in their friends. I hope they're as lucky as I am and find great pals.

© 1995 by John Wiley & Sons, Inc.

Name _____ **Date** _____

Great Friends
Revising and Writing a Final Copy

DIRECTIONS: Revise the draft of your essay about great friends. Here are some of the things you might look for to correct and/or change:

1. Is your grammar correct? Do all subjects and verbs agree?

2. Is your spelling correct? Check in the dictionary for any words that you are not sure of spelling.

3. Have you always used the best word or phrase to convey your meaning clearly? If you have used any vague words, such as *nice, okay, talk,* or *see,* replace them with something more specific.

4. Does your first paragraph clearly state the topic?

5. Do you give some interesting details that make your statements vivid to the reader?

6. Does your final paragraph sum up and conclude this essay?

When you finish your revisions, write your final copy on the lines below. (Use the back of this paper if you need more room.)

© 1995 by John Wiley & Sons, Inc.

GREAT FRIENDS

_____

_____

_____

_____

_____

_____

_____

_____

_____

Name _____ Date _____

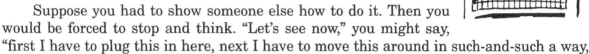

Here's How-To!
Prewriting

DIRECTIONS: When you know how to do something well, you don't usually think about each little step you must take. You just go ahead and do it.

Suppose you had to show someone else how to do it. Then you would be forced to stop and think. "Let's see now," you might say, "first I have to plug this in here, next I have to move this around in such-and-such a way, then . . ."

This is exactly what you will think about now because you are going to write a "how-to article." You are going to teach others how to do something that is new to them.

What do you know how to do? Can you program a VCR? Lots of people (especially adults) have trouble mastering that skill. Do you know how to bake brownies? Could you describe the game of baseball to someone who has never heard of it? Can you operate a computer? Do you build model airplanes? Have you studied ballet dancing?

Choose one of the skills mentioned above or any other that you know how to do and write down everything that comes into your mind about this procedure—any words, phrases, or sentences that might have anything to do with it. Don't worry about how you're going to use this information. Right now, you are just brainstorming—making a list of data. Later, you'll decide what to use and what to discard. First complete the title below. Then, write your brainstorming list on the lines underneath.

HOW-TO   **A**

_____

_____

_____

_____

_____

_____

_____

_____

_____

© 1995 by John Wiley & Sons, Inc.

Name _____ **Date** _____

Here's How-To!
First Draft

DIRECTIONS: Your "how to" essay will be divided into three sections.

The first paragraph will introduce the topic and tell a little about it, as in this example:

> Doesn't everybody love chocolate pudding? Chocolate cream pie is mostly chocolate pudding, but it also has a tasty pie crust and even yummier whipped cream. It is easy to prepare.

The main body of the essay tells how to do it. Describe the procedure in the order in which it is done. Be clear. Give all necessary details about each step. This part of the essay will consist of several paragraphs, probably two or three, perhaps more. Each paragraph can contain several steps. A step that is long and detailed might require a whole paragraph to itself. In this example, note the use of transitional words, such as next and then, to move smoothly from step to step:

> The first step is to prepare a pie crust. You can make one from scratch, but it is easier to use a frozen 9-inch crust from the frozen foods section of your supermarket. Follow the directions on the package. Usually, it just has to be baked in a preheated 400° oven for 10 minutes.
> Next, prepare one package of chocolate pudding mix. I usually use My-T-Fine® or Jell-O® brand. Follow the directions on the box. Put the mix into a saucepan and stir in 2 cups of milk. Heat at medium heat, stirring frequently, until it comes to a boil. Remove from heat and cool for 5 minutes.
> Pour the chocolate pudding into the baked pie crust. Then, cool in the refrigerator for several hours. Add prepared whipped cream, such as Reddi Whip®, just before serving.

The last paragraph of the how-to essay repeats the topic and concludes it in an interesting manner, as in the example below:

> Your family will love you when you serve this chocolate cream pie. They will be impressed with your cooking skill and never suspect how easy it is to prepare this tasty dessert.

Write a first draft, using the structure described above. Since this is only a draft, don't worry about spelling or grammar. Concentrate on getting your thoughts down on paper. Begin on the lines below and use the back of this paper if necessary.

_____

_____

_____

_____

© 1995 by John Wiley & Sons, Inc.

Name _____ **Date** _____

Here's How-To!
Revising and Writing a Final Copy

DIRECTIONS: Correct and revise your draft, making corrections and changes right on the copy. Use these guidelines when revising:

1. Is your grammar correct? Are all sentences complete? Do subjects and verbs agree? Watch for run-on sentences.

2. Check your spelling in a dictionary.

3. Is your subject stated in the first paragraph? Do you describe it in a way that will make the reader want to go on? Beginning with a question or with something humorous is always effective. Make any changes here that will make for a more interesting beginning.

4. Are the steps of your "how-to" stated in a logical step-by-step manner? If you have skipped around anywhere, change that now! Have you given every detail that is necessary to do this successfully? Are your descriptions clear and easy to follow? If there is anything that a reader may not understand, change that now.

5. Have you used transitional words, such as *then, now, next,* and *finally,* to make smooth transitions from one step to the next?

6. Does your last paragraph restate the topic and conclude it in an interesting manner? Can you think of a way to end it with more of a bang?

   When you are certain your essay is as good as you can make it, fill in the title and write your final copy below. (Use the back of this paper if you need more room.)

HOW-TO   **A**

_____

_____

_____

_____

_____

_____

_____

© 1995 by John Wiley & Sons, Inc.

Name _____ **Date** _____

Magic Wishes
Prewriting

In legends and fairy tales, the hero or heroine is sometimes granted three wishes. This doesn't usually happen in real life. Not until now! In this essay, you are going to use a dose of fairy tale magic!

What would you wish for if you could have three wishes that would come true? You don't want to choose carelessly because you might leave out something truly important. Suppose you didn't think of the one thing you wanted most of all until the fourth wish! Wouldn't you be sorry?

This is where making a list comes in handy! Give a lot of thought to this brainstorming list before you commit yourself to the three wishes.

DIRECTIONS:

1. Write your first wish next to "Wish #1" below. Underneath that, list your reasons for wanting this and how it would make your life (or the lives of others) better. This is just your worksheet, so you don't have to use complete sentences—words and phrases should be enough.

2. Write your second wish next to "Wish #2" below. Follow the same procedure as above.

3. Write your third wish next to "Wish # 3" below. Follow the same procedure as above.

© 1995 by John Wiley & Sons, Inc.

BRAINSTORMING LIST

Wish #1: _____

_____

_____

Wish #2: _____

_____

_____

Wish #3: _____

_____

_____

Name _____ Date _____

Magic Wishes
First Draft

This essay will be easy to write if you divide it into three sections.

SECTION ONE: The first paragraph will introduce the topic and tell a little about it. Here is one example:

> Do wishes ever come true? It happens in stories and fairy tales. Maybe it could happen in real life, too. There are three things I would wish for most if I had the chance.

DIRECTIONS: On a separate paper, write your name, date, and the title "Magic Wishes—First Draft." Write a first paragraph introducing the topic. You can be humorous or mysterious or just factual. This is only a draft, so don't worry about spelling or grammar. Just get down your ideas. Your introduction should contain at least three sentences.

SECTION TWO: The main part of the essay will describe your wishes. Use one paragraph for each wish. State the wish, then add several sentences describing your reasons for wishing this and what the results might be. Since there are three wishes, there will be three paragraphs in this section, as in the following example.

> My first wish is for my dad to win the state lottery. Not just any lottery will do. I want him to win it when it gets up to about 10 million dollars. Then, we'll be rich! We'll be able to buy anything we want.

> My second wish is to become a rock star. I'd like this to happen by the time I'm 16. I'd be part of a really cool group and travel all around the world.

> I have to admit that my first two wishes are selfish. That's why my third wish is for everybody. I wish that everyone in the world could have a nice house, enough food, and live in a free country like the United States.

DIRECTIONS: Write the main section of your essay on your paper after the first paragraph. Set it up like the one above. Use the information from your brainstorming list. Remember, this is just a draft! There will be three paragraphs in this section.

SECTION THREE: The last paragraph of the essay restates the topic and comments on it. This is a good place to show your feelings about these wishes and their chances of coming true, as in this example.

> I wish I could wave a wand and make these three wishes come true. But I can't! All I can do is hope. Maybe there really is such a thing as magic. After all, nothing is impossible!

DIRECTIONS: Write a concluding paragraph at the end of your first draft. It should contain at least three sentences. It is best to continue the tone you began in the introduction, whether humorous, mysterious, or factual.

© 1995 by John Wiley & Sons, Inc.

Name _____ Date _____

Magic Wishes
Revising and Writing a Final Copy

DIRECTIONS: Correct and revise your draft right on the copy.

1. Is your grammar correct? Do subjects and verbs agree? Are your sentences complete?

2. Check spelling in a dictionary.

3. Is the subject stated effectively in the first paragraph? Can you make the introduction more interesting?

4. Are there three paragraphs in the main section of your essay? Does each paragraph discuss one wish in an exciting way?

5. Does your concluding paragraph restate the topic and sum up your thoughts about it?

When you are sure that your essay is as good as you can make it, write your final copy below. Indent at the beginning of each paragraph. (Use the back of this paper if necessary.)

MAGIC WISHES

_____

_____

_____

_____

_____

_____

_____

_____

_____

_____

_____

© 1995 by John Wiley & Sons, Inc.

Name _____   Date _____

The Best Season of the Year
Prewriting

Each season has pluses and minuses. Which do you like best? It's different for different people. Ski nuts prefer winter. Sun worshippers love summer. You are going to describe your favorite season and give three reasons for liking it best.

A brainstorming list will help you organize your thoughts in a way that will make it easy to write this essay.

DIRECTIONS:

1. On the first line of your brainstorming list, write down your favorite season. Next to that, put down all the words and phrases that come into your head to describe that time of year.

2. Next to "Reason #1," write a sentence stating once reason for liking this season best. Then, on the lines below, write some words and phrases that will help develop that statement.

3. Next to "Reason #2," write a sentence stating your second reason. Then, on the lines below, write words and phrases that will help develop that statement.

4. Next to "Reason #3," write a sentence stating your third reason. Then, on the line below, write words and phrases that will help develop that statement.

BRAINSTORMING LIST

Favorite Season: _____

_____

Reason #1: _____

_____

Reason #2: _____

_____

Reason #3: _____

_____

© 1995 by John Wiley & Sons, Inc.

Name _____ **Date** _____

The Best Season of the Year
First Draft

Your brainstorming list will make it easy for you to produce a clear, well-written essay. The more information on your brainstorming list, the more choices you'll have to include in the first draft of your essay.

DIRECTIONS: On a separate sheet of paper, write your name, date, and the title, "The Best Season of the Year—First Draft."

Your first paragraph will introduce the topic. The sentence you wrote on your brainstorming list next to "Favorite Season" can be the first or last sentence. Add several sentences describing your chosen season. Use the words and phrases on your brainstorming list as a guide. Don't worry about spelling or grammar in this draft. Just get down your ideas in three sentences or more. Here is an example:

> Lots of people hate winter. They complain about the cold and the snow. Not me. I love winter. I think it's the best season of the year.

The next three paragraphs will develop your topic. "Reason #1" on your brainstorming list can be used in the first sentence. Develop this statement using the words and phrases on your list. Do the same in separate paragraphs for "Reason #2" and "Reason #3." Each paragraph should have at least three sentences. Write this first draft below your first paragraph.

The last (fifth) paragraph restates the topic and comments on it, as in the example below.

> I don't care how many complaints I hear about my favorite season. I love the cold, the snow, and the ice. I'll always like winter best.

That's how easy it is to write the first draft of your final paragraph when you prepare a well-organized *brainstorming list* first.

© 1995 by John Wiley & Sons, Inc.

Name _____   Date _____

The Best Season of the Year
Revising and Writing a Final Copy

DIRECTIONS: Correct and revise your first draft. Use the following guidelines:

1. Is your grammar correct? Do subjects and verbs agree? Are your sentences complete?

2. Check spelling in a dictionary.

3. Is the topic stated effectively in the first paragraph? Can you make the introduction more interesting?

4. Are there three paragraphs in the main section of your essay? Does each paragraph begin with a sentence stating one reason?

5. Does your concluding paragraph restate the topic and sum it up in an interesting way?

When you are sure your essay is as good as you can make it, write your final copy below. Indent at the beginning of each paragraph. (Use the back of this paper if necessary.)

THE BEST SEASON OF THE YEAR

_____

_____

_____

_____

_____

_____

_____

_____

_____

_____

© 1995 by John Wiley & Sons, Inc.

Name _____   Date _____

Music! Music! Music!
Prewriting

You don't have to be a musician to have an interest in music. Most people enjoy music. Some have favorites like rock, rap, heavy metal, jazz, country, classical, or some combination. There are music lovers who like all kinds. You don't have to be an expert to write an essay about music, especially if you first prepare a brainstorming list.

DIRECTIONS: First decide upon your essay's point of view. Do you want to write about music in general? Or would you prefer to describe your own personal musical tastes? Or do you want to write about one type of music? Or do you tell about an instrument or instruments and the kinds of music they can produce, or about certain bands or groups? Choose one of these points of view and write it on the line below.

POINT OF VIEW: _____

Keep this point of view in mind when preparing your brainstorming list, as directed below.

BRAINSTORMING LIST

Write a sentence for your introduction that indicates your point of view: _____

_____

_____

List three or four main points of your essay. These can be the types of music, instruments, or groups you are writing about. If you decide to write about only one type of music, you can list details such as groups, performers, or songs. Write each point on a separate line. _____

_____

_____

Next to each point on the lines above, write some words or phrases that can be used in developing this point.

On the lines below, write some thoughts you can include in your final paragraph. _____

_____

© 1995 by John Wiley & Sons, Inc.

Name _____   Date _____

Music! Music! Music!
First Draft

Keep your brainstorming list in front of you. It will make your first draft easy to write.

DIRECTIONS: On a separate paper, write your name, date, and the title, "Music! Music! Music!—First Draft."

Your first paragraph will introduce the topic. You can use the introductory sentence from your brainstorming list, then develop it with two or three additional sentences, as in this example.

> I must be an oddball. All my friends are into rock or rap or heavy metal. Not me! It's embarrassing to admit this, but I love country music.

The first paragraph should contain at least three sentences. This is only a draft, so just concentrate on putting down your thoughts.

The next section of your essay will contain one paragraph for each of the points you wrote down on your brainstorming list. That will make a total of three or four paragraphs in this section. Begin each paragraph with one statement from your list. Follow this with several sentences developing this statement. The words and phrases on your brainstorming list will come in handy. Each paragraph should contain at least three or four sentences.

The last paragraph will restate and sum up your topic. Use the concluding thoughts from your brainstorming list. The last paragraph should have at least three sentences, as in this example.

> Now you know why I like country music so much. I suppose it's a taste I inherited, but I'm stuck with it. What's more, I wouldn't trade it for any other music in the world.

© 1995 by John Wiley & Sons, Inc.

Name _____ **Date** _____

Music! Music! Music!

Revising and Writing a Final Copy

DIRECTIONS: Correct and revise your draft. Follow these guidelines:

1. Are your sentences complete? Do subjects and verbs agree?

2. Check spelling in a dictionary.

3. Does your first paragraph state the topic? Is it as interesting as you can make it? Are there at least three sentences in this paragraph?

4. Are there three or four paragraphs in the main section of your essay? Does each paragraph state and develop one point?

5. Do you restate and sum up the topic in your last paragraph?

When you are sure that your essay is as good as you can make it, write your final copy below. Indent at the beginning of each paragraph. (Use the back of this paper if necessary.)

MUSIC! MUSIC! MUSIC!

_____

_____

_____

_____

_____

_____

_____

_____

_____

_____

_____

_____

© 1995 by John Wiley & Sons, Inc.

Name _____ **Date** _____

My Favorite Things
Prewriting

What are your favorite activities? In this essay, you are going to describe three of the things you like doing best. When you are finished, it will be fun to compare your essay with those of your classmates and see how alike or different they are.

This should be an easy essay to write, but, even so, a brainstorming list will be of great help.

DIRECTIONS:

1. On the lines below, write at least one sentence you can use to introduce this topic in your first paragraph. Follow this with a list of words or phrases that might be useful in developing this introduction.

_____

_____

2. Next to "Activity #1," write a sentence stating the first activity you enjoy. Follow this with a list of words or phrases that will be useful in describing this activity. Do the same thing for "Activity #2," and "Activity #3."

Activity #1: _____

_____

Activity #2: _____

_____

Activity #3: _____

_____

3. On the lines below, write some thoughts (words, phrases, or sentences) that can be used in your concluding paragraph.

_____

_____

© 1995 by John Wiley & Sons, Inc.

Name _____   Date _____

My Favorite Things
First Draft

If you followed the directions for Activity 63A, this essay will practically write itself! Just use your brainstorming list and the following directions as guides.

DIRECTIONS:

1. On a separate paper, write your name, date, and the title, "My Favorite Things—First Draft."

2. Write the first paragraph using the topic sentence from your brainstorming list. Expand this introduction making use of the words and phrases on your list, as in this example.

> Wouldn't life be great if we never had to do things we dislike? If I could spend all my time in enjoyable activities, I'd sure be a happy camper. Then I could have fun with my favorite things.

The first paragraph should contain at least three sentences. Remember, this is only a draft. Just concentrate on getting down your ideas.

3. The next section of your essay will contain one paragraph for each of your favorite activities. You already have the topic sentence of each paragraph on your brainstorming list. Copy it down. Then, for each paragraph, follow with at least two or three additional sentences developing this topic. Describe the activity and tell what you like about it. There will be three paragraphs in this section of the essay.

4. The last paragraph will restate and sum up your topic. Use the concluding thoughts from your brainstorming list. The last paragraph should have at least three sentences, as in this example.

> Of course, it's not possible. I know it is just a dream. But I can't help thinking that life would be grand if I could spend each day biking, swimming, and playing with video games.

© 1995 by John Wiley & Sons, Inc.

Name _____ **Date** _____

My Favorite Things
Revising and Writing a Final Copy

DIRECTIONS: Correct and revise your draft. Follow these guidelines:

1. Are your sentences complete? Do subjects and verbs agree?

2. Check spelling in a dictionary.

3. Does your first paragraph state the topic? Is it as clear and interesting as you can make it? Are there at least three sentences in this paragraph?

4. Are there three paragraphs in the main section of your essay? Does each paragraph state and develop one activity?

5. Do you restate and sum up in your last paragraph?

When you are satisfied with your revised essay, write your final copy below. Indent at the beginning of each paragraph. (Use the back of this paper if necessary.)

MY FAVORITE THINGS

_____

_____

_____

_____

_____

_____

_____

_____

_____

_____

_____

_____

© 1995 by John Wiley & Sons, Inc.

Name _____   **Date** _____

Making Better Schools
Prewriting

Adults spend a lot of time in meetings and discussions, trying to figure out how to make your schools better. They seek advice from all sorts of experts. The only opinions that usually are not heard are from those most concerned—you, the students!

Here is your chance to make your voice heard. Give serious thought to ways in which your schools can be improved. Use this brainstorming list to write down and organize your ideas in a convincing way.

DIRECTIONS:

1. In this essay, you will make three suggestions for improving your schools. Write down your three ideas in sentence form below.

1. _____

2. _____

3. _____

2. The brainstorming list below is divided into three sections.

Next to 1, write words, phrases, or sentences that could be used to develop your first suggestion.

Next to 2, write words, phrases, or sentences for developing your second suggestion.

Next to 3, list words, phrases, or sentences about your third suggestion.

BRAINSTORMING LIST

1. _____

_____

2. _____

_____

3. _____

_____

© 1995 by John Wiley & Sons, Inc.

Name _____   Date _____

Making Better Schools
First Draft

Keep your brainstorming list handy. It will make your first draft easy to write.

DIRECTIONS:

1. On a separate paper, write your name, date, and the title, "Making Better Schools—First Draft."

2. Your first paragraph will introduce the topic. Write an interesting topic sentence. Follow with several additional sentences giving reasons why your opinion is important, as in this example.

> Students are interested in having good schools. After all, it's where we spend most of our time. Most of us have definite opinions about how we can have better schools. Here are some of my ideas.

The first paragraph should contain at least three sentences. This is only a draft, so just concentrate on getting down your thoughts.

3. The main section will contain three paragraphs, one for each of your suggestions. You can use the three statements on your brainstorming list as the first sentence of each paragraph. Follow up with reasons why this is a good idea. Each of these paragraphs should contain at least three sentences.

4. The last paragraph will restate and sum up your topic in two or three sentences, as in this example.

> Kids are the ones most affected by our schools. We want the best for ourselves and our futures. That's why our opinions should be taken seriously.

© 1995 by John Wiley & Sons, Inc.

Name _____   **Date** _____

Making Better Schools
Revising and Writing a Final Copy

DIRECTIONS: Correct and revise your draft. Follow these guidelines:

1. Are your sentences complete? Do subjects and verbs agree?

2. Check spelling in a dictionary.

3. Does your first paragraph state the topic? Is it as clear and interesting as you can make it?

4. In the next three paragraphs, are your suggestions stated logically? Do you clearly describe each one? Do you offer convincing reasons for them?

5. Does your last paragraph restate and sum up the topic?

When you are sure that your essay is as good as you can make it, write your final copy below. Indent at the beginning of each paragraph. (Use the back of this paper if necessary.)

MAKING BETTER SCHOOLS

_____

_____

_____

_____

_____

_____

_____

_____

_____

_____

_____

_____

_____

© 1995 by John Wiley & Sons, Inc.

Name _____ Date _____

Who Collects Stamps?
Prewriting—Research

Research means looking for facts like a detective. It can be fun, as you will discover in this activity.

Most people have hobbies—things they do for enjoyment. A hobby can be ordinary like reading or unusual like breeding snakes. What are your hobbies? Write them on the line below.

My hobbies: _____

Wouldn't it be interesting to know how many others share your hobbies and what other hobbies are popular with kids? It's easy to find out. Just ask! In fact, that's how you're going to do your research for this project. You're going to ask people about their hobbies and why they like them. This kind of research is called interviewing.

DIRECTIONS:

1. Talk to at least 10 kids in your class or school. Ask them two questions: (1) What is your favorite hobby? (2) What is it that you like about this activity?

2. Use this worksheet to record your interviews. In the first column below, write the person's name. Put his or her hobby in the second column. In the third column, write down why he or she likes this activity.

RESEARCH NOTES: INTERVIEWS

NAME	*HOBBY*	*WHY THEY LIKE IT*

© 1995 by John Wiley & Sons, Inc.

Name _____ **Date** _____

Who Collects Stamps?
Prewriting—Organizing Information

The information you need for this essay is on your research sheet. Now you must organize these facts, as directed below.

DIRECTIONS:

1. Count the number of times each hobby is mentioned on your research sheet. Choose the ones that are mentioned more than once. List them below, followed by the number of people who mention them.

© 1995 by John Wiley & Sons, Inc.

HOBBY	*NUMBER OF PEOPLE*
_____	_____
_____	_____
_____	_____
_____	_____
_____	_____
_____	_____
_____	_____
_____	_____

2. List below the two hobbies most often named.

_____

3. Write a sentence that could be used to introduce this topic based on your information, such as "You'd be surprised at some of the weird activities kids in this school enjoy," or "Hobbies such as stamp collecting are as popular as ever." Write your topic sentence here.

_____

4. Look through your research worksheet. Choose the most interesting comment made about each of the two hobbies you listed above, and write them here.

" _____ "

" _____ "

5. List several unusual hobbies named on your research worksheet and some that only one person liked.

_____

_____

6. Did anything you found out surprise you? What?

_____

© 1995 by John Wiley & Sons, Inc.

Name _____   Date _____

Who Collects Stamps?
First Draft

You should be able to write a first draft easily from the information you wrote on Activity 65B. It may or may not be necessary to consult with your research notes on Activity 65A.

DIRECTIONS:

1. On a separate paper, write your name, date, and the title, "Who Collects Stamps?—First Draft."

2. Your first paragraph will introduce the topic. Use the topic sentence on your worksheet. Expand upon it in any way you want. You can talk about the subject of hobbies in general or tell how you got your facts or even begin with something amusing one of the kids said like, "What's a hobby?" Here is an example.

> "Who's got time for hobbies?" This was one classmate's reaction to the question, "What's your favorite hobby?" This poor, overorganized soul may be surprised to learn that most kids still have hobbies they love.

The first paragraph should have at least three sentences. This is only a draft, so concentrate on getting down your thoughts.

3. The main section will contain three paragraphs. In the first of these paragraphs, describe one of the most popular hobbies. Tell how many kids enjoy it. Use a quote about it. Do the same for the other popular hobby in the next paragraph. The third paragraph in this section can be used to list and describe some of the other popular hobbies and some that aren't popular at all. Each of these paragraphs should contain at least three sentences.

4. The last paragraph will restate and sum up the topic. This would be a good place to state any conclusion, such as why certain hobbies are popular and others are not. Or you can tell why it is important for kids to have hobbies. Here is an example of a concluding paragraph.

> You can tell a lot about a person from what they enjoy doing. You might be surprised at a classmate's hobby or it might be just what you expected. Sometimes hobbies can grow into what we'll be later in life. Even if they don't, they provide many happy hours.

© 1995 by John Wiley & Sons, Inc.

Name _____ **Date** _____

Who Collects Stamps?
Revising and Writing a Final Copy

DIRECTIONS: Correct and revise your draft. Follow these guidelines:

1. Are your sentences complete? Do subjects and verbs agree?

2. Check spelling in a dictionary.

3. Does your first paragraph state the topic in a clear and interesting way? Are there at least three sentences in this paragraph?

4. Are there three paragraphs in the main section of your essay? Do two of these paragraphs name and describe one popular hobby? Does the third one summarize some other interesting facts about this topic?

5. Do you restate and perhaps come to a conclusion in the last paragraph?

When you are satisfied with your revised essay, write your final copy below. Indent at the beginning of each paragraph. (Use the back of this paper if necessary.)

WHO COLLECTS STAMPS?

_____

_____

_____

_____

_____

_____

_____

_____

_____

_____

© 1995 by John Wiley & Sons, Inc.

Name _____   Date _____

The Amazing Man From Milwaukee
Prewriting—Research Worksheet

Here are a whole bunch of facts about a man named Christopher Latham Sholes.

1. Christopher Latham Sholes was the inventor of the typewriter.

2. He was born in a log farmhouse in Milwaukee, Wisconsin, in 1819.

3. When he was a boy, people called him a "dreamer." He loved to take things apart and put them together again.

4. He was a printer by profession.

5. He began to learn the printing trade as an apprentice at the age of 14.

6. At the age of 19, he became editor of a newspaper, the *Wisconsin State Journal*.

7. He also worked as a postmaster in Milwaukee.

8. His hobby was working on inventions.

9. One of his inventions was a machine that could automatically put numbers on sets of railway tickets or on the pages of a book.

10. In the 1860s Sholes became interested in "writing machines." At that time, people wrote only with pens or pencils.

11. A lot of inventors had tried to make "writing machines," but none of them worked.

12. Sholes began to spend all his free time working on this invention.

13. His friend, Samuel Soule, helped him.

14. For a long time, none of the machines they designed worked.

15. Soule wanted to give up, but Sholes kept working stubbornly.

16. In 1867, Sholes finally constructed a machine that could write all the letters of the alphabet and could operate faster than a person writing with a pen.

17. He called it a "Type-writer."

18. The first message typed on this machine was, "C. LATHAM SHOLES SEPTEMBER 1867."

19. The first type-writer model kept breaking down.

20. Here are some of the problems he had. The typebars jammed. The hand-inked ribbon was sticky and messy. The string that held the carriage together kept breaking.

21. Sholes quit his other jobs and spent all his time working on his invention. He had to borrow money to keep going.

© 1995 by John Wiley & Sons, Inc.

22. It took six more years for Sholes to build a typewriter that worked well enough to be used by anyone.

23. In 1873, Sholes was finally able to build a typewriter that really worked well. The first thing he typed on it was, "DEAR FRIEND—THIS IS A WRITING MACHINE BY WHICH WORDS CAN BE WRITTEN EASILY AND READ BY ALL."

24. Sholes sold all his rights to the typewriter to the Remington Company for $6,000. Later, the company would earn many millions.

25. After he invented the typewriter, Sholes never used a pen or pencil again. He typed everything, even his signature.

26. Christopher Latham Sholes has been called "the world's most unknown inventor."

27. If it wasn't for Sholes's invention, we might never have the word processors and computers we use today.

© 1995 by John Wiley & Sons, Inc.

Name _____   Date _____

The Amazing Man From Milwaukee
Prewriting—Organizing Information

It will be easy to write an essay about the man who invented the typewriter if you first follow these directions for selecting and organizing the facts.

DIRECTIONS:

1. Look over the facts on your research worksheet. Decide which facts should appear in your introductory paragraph. Copy these on the lines below. Include a topic sentence for your essay based on what you have learned from the research.

_____

_____

_____

2. Read the research information again and choose two main facts that seem most important. Write a sentence about one of these below. Under that, copy some of the other information that could be used in a paragraph about this main fact.

_____

_____

_____

3. Do the same for the second main fact.

_____

_____

_____

4. On the lines below, copy some additional information you want to include in your essay about Christopher Latham Sholes.

_____

_____

_____

© 1995 by John Wiley & Sons, Inc.

Name _____ **Date** _____

The Amazing Man From Milwaukee
First Draft

© 1995 by John Wiley & Sons, Inc.

It should be easy to write this essay from Activity 66B. It may sometimes be helpful to refer to Activity 66A. Keep both worksheets handy.

DIRECTIONS:

1. On a separate paper, write your name, date, and the title, "The Amazing Man From Milwaukee—First Draft."

2. Your first paragraph will introduce the subject. Use the topic sentence from your worksheet. Develop the introduction with other thoughts or information, as in this example.

> He has been called "the world's most unknown inventor." His name was Christopher Latham Sholes. In 1873, he invented a machine he called the typewriter.

3. The main section of your essay will contain three paragraphs. The first of these will be about your first main fact. Copy the topic sentence you have already written for this paragraph. Follow up with at least two more sentences, including related facts. Begin the next paragraph with the topic sentence you have already written about the second main fact. Add at least two more sentences with related facts. In the third paragraph in this section, include other facts about the inventor and/or the invention.

4. The last paragraph will restate and sum up your topic in two or three sentences. This would be a good place to state why this invention was so important, as in this example.

> The typewriter was one of the most important machines ever invented. It speeded up the paperwork that was important for business and personal use, and led to our modern-day word processors and computers.

Name _____ **Date** _____

The Amazing Man From Milwaukee
Revising and Writing a Final Copy

DIRECTIONS: Correct and revise your draft. Follow these guidelines:

1. Are your sentences complete? Do subjects and verbs agree?

2. Check spelling in a dictionary.

3. Does your first paragraph state the topic? Is it as clear and interesting as you can make it? Are there at least three sentences in this paragraph?

4. Are there three paragraphs in the main section of your essay? Do each of the first two of these paragraphs state one main fact, followed by other information that supports it? Does the third paragraph in this section offer other interesting, appropriate information? Are there at least three sentences in each paragraph?

5. Do you sum up the topic in your last paragraph? Do you help the reader recognize the importance of this subject?

When you are satisfied with your revised essay, write your final copy below. Indent at the beginning of each paragraph. (Use the back of this paper if necessary.)

© 1995 by John Wiley & Sons, Inc.

THE AMAZING MAN FROM MILWAUKEE

_____

_____

_____

_____

_____

_____

_____

_____

_____

© 1995 by John Wiley & Sons, Inc.

Name _____ **Date** _____

Best Foot Forward
Prewriting

Everybody has both good and bad qualities. Sometimes it is important to emphasize your good side—to put your "best foot forward."

You try to do this with new teachers at the beginning of a school year or when meeting new friends. There are lots of situations in which you want people to see you at your best. As you get older, there will be even more of these—applying for a job, going to school interviews, getting to know fellow workers, and meeting with supervisors or customers. In this essay, you are going to present yourself in a positive way, concentrating on your good points. This brainstorming list will help.

DIRECTIONS:

1. Character and personality—In the first column below, list positive aspects of your character and personality (kindness, honesty, loyalty, originality, perseverance, hardworking, patient, imaginative, reliability, promptness, cheerful, friendliness, ability to work well with others, and so on). Be truthful! In the second column, next to each one, list an example of how you apply this in your life.

CHARACTER / PERSONALITY TRAIT   *EXAMPLE*

_____   _____

_____   _____

_____   _____

_____   _____

2. Abilities and skills—In the first column below, list your abilities and skills (intelligence, ability to follow directions, creativity, physical strength, athletic skill, math or language skills, mechanical ability, problem-solving, leadership, good cook, good listener, acting or dancing ability, musical skills, and so on). Be truthful! In the second column, next to each, give an example of how this has been useful.

ABILITIES / SKILLS   *EXAMPLE OF USEFULNESS*

_____   _____

_____   _____

_____   _____

_____   _____

Name _____   **Date** _____

Best Foot Forward
First Draft

Your brainstorming list will help you write this essay. Don't feel funny about writing good things about yourself. Just be truthful. If it seems embarrassing, pretend someone else is writing about you.

DIRECTIONS:

1. On a separate paper, write your name, date, and the title, "Best Foot Forward—First Draft."

2. Your first paragraph will introduce the subject. It can be factual, mysterious, or humorous, as in the following example.

> Everyone has faults, even me, if you can believe that! However, you're not going to hear about any of those now. I'm going to put my best foot forward.

Your first paragraph should have at least three sentences. Remember, this is just a first draft.

3. The main section of your essay will contain two paragraphs. The first one will discuss your positive personality and character traits. Choose several of these from your brainstorming list. Follow each one with an active description from the second column of your brainstorming list. Discuss your abilities and skills in the next paragraph. Choose two or three from your brainstorming list. Follow each with a description from the second column of your list.

4. The last paragraph will restate and sum up your topic in two or three sentences. You might want to include how it feels to be writing about yourself. Here is an example.

> It's not easy to write about yourself! I hope that I've succeeded in being honest. At least, anyone who reads this will know all that's best about me. Who knows? Maybe I'll be able to live up to it, after all!

© 1995 by John Wiley & Sons, Inc.

Name _____   Date _____

Best Foot Forward
Revising and Writing a Final Copy

DIRECTIONS: Correct and revise your draft. Follow these guidelines:

1. Are your sentences complete? Do subjects and verbs agree?

2. Check spelling in a dictionary.

3. Does your first paragraph state the topic in a clear and interesting way? Are there at least three sentences in this paragraph?

4. Are there two paragraphs in the main section of your essay? Does each paragraph have a clear topic sentence, followed by a statement of several traits or abilities and examples of their application?

5. Do you restate and sum up the topic and the essay in your last paragraph?

When you are satisfied with your revised essay, write your final copy below. Indent at the beginning of each paragraph. (Use the back of this paper if necessary.)

BEST FOOT FORWARD

_____

_____

_____

_____

_____

_____

_____

_____

_____

_____

© 1995 by John Wiley & Sons, Inc.

Name _____ **Date** _____

Something Great!
Prewriting

Every day on TV and in newspapers, advertisers try to convince us that what they are selling is great. Could you describe a product in a way that will make people want to have it? Wouldn't it be fun to do this with something that is familiar—something that most of us take for granted? Here are some of the ordinary objects you could describe: a bicycle, a sled, a computer, a dictionary, a camera, a clock, a TV set, an air conditioner, an automobile, an airplane, a lawn mower, or a telephone. Choose one of these (or another familiar product) and write it on the line below.

_____

The brainstorming list below is divided into two columns. In the first column, list all the words and phrases you can use to describe your product. In the second column, list words and phrases that tell in what ways it is useful. Use vivid language, such as sensory words (touch, sight, smell, hearing, and taste) and active verbs.

BRAINSTORMING LIST

DESCRIPTION	USES
_____	_____
_____	_____
_____	_____
_____	_____
_____	_____
_____	_____
_____	_____
_____	_____

© 1995 by John Wiley & Sons, Inc.

Name _____ Date _____

Something Great!
First Draft

© 1995 by John Wiley & Sons, Inc.

You are going to describe a product or object in a way that will make it seem exciting and desirable. It is important to use lots of vivid language. The sensory words and strong, active verbs you wrote on your brainstorming list will help you do this.

DIRECTIONS:

1. On a separate paper, write your name, date, and the title, "Something Great!—First Draft."

2. Your first paragraph will introduce the subject. The introduction should make the reader want to continue. It's often interesting to begin with a question or with a startling statement. Here is an example.

> It doesn't seem possible, but there was a time when people didn't own TV's. This wasn't even as far back as the stone age. My grandmother says that when she was a small child, there was no such thing as TV. Can you believe it? Could you live without your TV?

Your first paragraph should have at least three sentences.

3. The main section of your essay will contain two paragraphs. The first paragraph will describe its appearance. Pretend you are describing this object to someone who has never seen it before. Refer to more than one sense in your description of its color, shape, smell, taste, and movement. In the next paragraph, describe how this is used in a way that will make the reader want to own it. Use vivid language and active verbs to make it exciting and desirable. Each paragraph should have at least three sentences.

4. The last paragraph will restate and sum up your topic. Try to emphasize again how great it is. Here is an example.

> A TV set is absolutely necessary in today's world. It keeps you up to date on everything you need to know about what's going on in the world. It also provides many hours of fun for the whole family. No home should be without it!

Name _____   Date _____

Something Great!
Revising and Writing a Final Copy

DIRECTIONS: Correct and revise your draft. Follow these guidelines:

1. Are your sentences complete? Do subjects and verbs agree?

2. Check spelling in a dictionary.

3. Does your first paragraph state the topic in a clear and interesting way? Are there at least three sentences in this paragraph?

4. Are there two paragraphs in the main section of your essay? Does the first of these paragraphs describe the product vividly, using sensory language? Have you used active verbs in the next paragraph to show the product being used in an exciting way? Are there at least three sentences in each paragraph?

5. Does the last paragraph restate the subject interestingly?

    When you are satisfied with your revised essay, write your final copy below. Indent at the beginning of each paragraph. (Use the back of this paper if necessary.)

© 1995 by John Wiley & Sons, Inc.

SOMETHING GREAT

_____

_____

_____

_____

_____

_____

_____

_____

_____

_____

_____

Name _____ **Date** _____

Don't You Agree?
Prewriting

"Hey! Let's do this!" "No, let's do that!" "That's no fun. I'd rather do something else!"

Does this ever happen when you and your friends get together? How do you decide? Is one of you able to convince the others? How?

In this essay, you are going to convince others of the rightness of your opinion. Do you agree or disagree with these statements?

Schools should be in session all year.
The most exciting team sport to play is baseball.
The most exciting team sport to watch is football.
It's better to have one best friend than to be part of a group.
Boys and girls are equal in every way.
Video games are a waste of time.
Smoking is stupid and bad for your health.

Select one of the above statements and write one or two sentences telling whether you agree or disagree. These can later be used as topic sentences in your essay. (If there is another subject you have strong feelings about, you can choose that instead.)

_____

_____

Use the brainstorming list below to write down your ideas supporting your opinion. List both general and specific statements. For example, a general statement would be, "It's important to be able to get along with lots of different people if you want to be successful in life." A specific example would be, "If one of my friends is sick or away, there is always someone else I can hang out with." You can use complete sentences or just phrases when brainstorming.

BRAINSTORMING LIST

_____

_____

_____

_____

_____

© 1995 by John Wiley & Sons, Inc.

Name _____   Date _____

Don't You Agree?
First Draft

When you are writing this essay, determine that you are going to convince the reader that you are right. If you keep that in mind and use the work you have already done on your brainstorming list, this activity will be a "piece of cake."

DIRECTIONS:

1. On a separate paper, write your name, date, and the title, "Don't You Agree?—First Draft."

2. Your first paragraph will introduce the subject. Be positive. Be definite. Build this paragraph around the topic sentence or sentences on your brainstorming list. Here is an example.

> Some kids stick to one another like glue. You'd think they were the only two people in the world. That's not for me. I'm much happier being part of a happy, fun-loving group.

Your first paragraph should have at least three sentences.

3. The main section of your essay will contain two or three paragraphs. Choose two or three of the best statements on your brainstorming list that support your opinion. Use these as the topic sentences of each paragraph. Develop each idea with examples in the rest of that paragraph.

4. The last paragraph will restate and sum up your topic. This should be the most convincing section of your essay. It is your last chance to persuade the reader to agree with you. Here is an example.

> It's not a good idea to have just one friend. It's important to learn how to get along with many different people. When you have a group of friends, life is more interesting and lots more exciting.

© 1995 by John Wiley & Sons, Inc.

Name _____ **Date** _____

Don't You Agree?
Revising and Writing a Final Copy

DIRECTIONS: Correct and revise your draft. Follow these guidelines:

1. Are your sentences complete? Do subjects and verbs agree?

2. Check spelling in a dictionary.

3. Does your first paragraph clearly state the topic? Is your tone definite and positive? Are there at least three sentences in this paragraph?

4. Does each paragraph in the main section state one fact to support your opinion? Do you develop this fact with specific examples?

5. Do you restate your opinion in the last paragraph in a positive and convincing way?

When you are satisfied with your revised essay, write your final copy below. Indent at the beginning of each paragraph. (Use the back of this paper if necessary.)

DON'T YOU AGREE?

_____

_____

_____

_____

_____

_____

_____

_____

_____

_____

_____

_____

© 1995 by John Wiley & Sons, Inc.

Name _____   Date _____

A Perfect World
Prewriting—Brainstorming

There are many wonders in this world. But it is far from perfect. Just look at a newspaper any day and it is clear that many things are wrong.

If you had a magic wand that would turn this into a better world, what would you change and how would you change it?

DIRECTIONS: Use the brainstorming list below to compile your ideas. In the first column, list the things you think are wrong with the world. In the second column, tell how you would change them. This is just a way to get your thoughts down on paper. It's not necessary to use complete sentences. Words, phrases, and sentence fragments are good enough.

BRAINSTORMING LIST

THINGS THAT ARE WRONG	*HOW I WOULD CHANGE THEM*
_____	_____
_____	_____
_____	_____
_____	_____
_____	_____
_____	_____
_____	_____
_____	_____
_____	_____
_____	_____
_____	_____

© 1995 by John Wiley & Sons, Inc.

Name _____ Date _____

A Perfect World
Prewriting—Outline (First Page)

It might seem as though making an outline is a lot of trouble. That's not true. When you prepare a good outline, your essay almost writes itself. An outline can be done quickly and help you turn out a clear and logical essay. Use your brainstorming list as your source.

DIRECTIONS:

1. On a separate paper, write your name, date, and the title, "A Perfect World—Outline." (See the next page for an illustration of an outline.)

2. Write the Roman numeral I. Next to it, write "Introduction." On the next line, write "A. Topic Sentence." Next to this, write a topic sentence for your first paragraph.
On the next line, write "B." Next to this, write a word or phrase that will develop your topic sentence.
On the next line, write "C." Next to this, write another word or phrase to develop the topic sentence.

3. Choose three items from the first column of your brainstorming list. These will be the points you will make in the main section of the essay.
Write the Roman numeral II. Next to it, copy the first point you are going to use from your brainstorming list.
On the next line, write "A." Next to this, write a word or phrase you can use to develop this point.
On the next line, write "B." Next to this, write another word or phrase you can use to develop this point.
On the next line, write "C." Next to this, write another word or phrase you can use to develop this point.
Write the Roman numeral III. Next to it, copy the second point you are going to use from your brainstorming list. Follow the same directions as above for A, B, and C.
Write the Roman numeral IV. Next to it, copy the third point you are going to use from your brainstorming list. Follow the same directions as above for A, B, and C.

4. Write "V. Conclusion."
On the next line, write "A." Next to this, write a phrase or sentence that restates the topic.
On the next line, write "B." Next to this, write another phrase or sentence that adds to your conclusion.

Compare your outline with the sample on the next page.

© 1995 by John Wiley & Sons, Inc.

Name _____   Date _____

A Perfect World
Prewriting—Outline (Second Page)

Your outline will look something like this:

I.   INTRODUCTION
A.   Many bad things happen in the world today.
B.   It doesn't have to be that way.
C.   We could change this into a perfect world.

II.   FIRST POINT—Hunger
A.   Many people don't have enough food.
B.   Even babies die from starvation.
C.   Well-fed people are healthier and happier.

III.   SECOND POINT—Ignorance
A.   In some parts of the world, there are no schools.
B.   Even in our country, some kids don't get a good education.
C.   A good education can lead to a better life.

IV.   THIRD POINT—Wars
A.   Lots of people are killed in wars.
B.   There should be other ways to settle arguments.
C.   If everyone refused to fight, wars would end.

V.   CONCLUSION
A.   This world could be better than it is.
B.   There would not be hunger, ignorance, or war in a perfect world.

© 1995 by John Wiley & Sons, Inc.

Name _____ Date _____

A Perfect World
First Draft

DIRECTIONS: Follow your outline to write an easy first draft of the essay. There will be five paragraphs, one for each of the numerals on your outline. Write your first draft below. Indent at the beginning of each paragraph. (Use the back of this paper if necessary.)

A PERFECT WORLD

_____
_____
_____
_____
_____
_____
_____
_____
_____
_____
_____
_____
_____
_____
_____
_____
_____

© 1995 by John Wiley & Sons, Inc.

Name _____ Date _____

A Perfect World
Revising and Writing a Final Copy

DIRECTIONS: Correct and revise your draft. Follow these guidelines:

1. Are your sentences complete? Do subjects and verbs agree?

2. Check spelling in a dictionary.

3. Are all of your thoughts expressed in clear and interesting language?

4. Does your first paragraph (I. on your outline) introduce the topic? Is it as interesting as you can make it?

5. Does each paragraph in the main section (II., III., and IV. on your outline) state and develop one aspect of your "perfect world"?

6. Does the last paragraph (V. on your outline) restate and sum up the topic? Is it as clear and interesting as you can make it?

When you are satisfied with your revised essay, write your final copy below. Indent at the beginning of each paragraph. (Use the back of this paper if necessary.)

© 1995 by John Wiley & Sons, Inc.

A PERFECT WORLD

_____

_____

_____

_____

_____

_____

_____

_____

_____

_____

UNIT FIVE

Simple Letters

For a long time, letter writing was considered to be a dying (if not already completely defunct) art. The telephone had become the preferred method of communication for the up-and-coming generations. It seems, however, that the obituaries may have been written too soon. Now, with the advent of computer networks, and most especially the fax machine, written communication is again gaining in favor. A 1994 article in the Book Review section of *The* Sunday *New York Times* noted this resurgence of interest in letter writing. The author of the article pointed out some advantages of this mode of communication, primarily the time it gives its practitioners to think reflexively, to meditate on ideas and their organization, and to change and alter the copy, which all lead to more fully expressive communication.

The new National Postal Museum in Washington, D.C., includes an entire gallery called, "The Art of Cards and Letters," displaying letters written from colonial times to the present. Obviously a strong interest exists for this mode of communication. Although the telephone still reigns supreme, more-advanced technology may help resurrect the practice of letter writing.

But are the skills there? They may have been lost for many, but there is no reason they cannot be regained. This unit is designed to convince even the most letter-phobic student that nothing could be easier than writing a letter. They will be encouraged to acquire letter-writing skills by completing activities that seem relevant to their lives, such as letters of invitation, thank-you letters, fan letters, pen pal messages, and so on. Other exercises stimulate the imagination, such as a letter from the twenty-first century or one to an owner from a pet. This variety in letter-writing activities makes it possible for the teacher to choose those that are most appropriate for particular classes and students.

Throughout, the steps of the writing process are emphasized, including prewriting, first drafts, revising, and writing final copy.

Name _____ Date _____

Party Time!
Prewriting

DIRECTIONS: Parties are fun! So is deciding whom to invite. It's easy enough to fill out a card with a time, date, and place. But if you really want to convince your guests to attend, why not send each one a personal letter of invitation? You can make them see how much fun they'll have and why you want them to be there. Wouldn't you like to get a letter like the one below?

> 21 Elm Street
> Milton, NY 12345
> October 20, 19__
>
> Dear Jonathan,
>
>   We're having a Halloween party at my house on Sunday, October 30. I'm inviting the whole gang on the block. We're going to play games and watch a scary video. It'll be great! You could wear your super skeleton costume. It won't be as much fun without you, so please come!
>
>   Your friend,

© 1995 by John Wiley & Sons, Inc.

Doesn't the writer make the party seem like fun? He also lets his friend know how much he's wanted. Not many people would refuse such an invitation.

    Think about a party you might like to have soon or at some time in the future. It can be for a birthday, Valentine's Day, Halloween, New Year's, or any other occasion. Make some notes on the lines below about what sort of party you would like, when it might take place, who you'll invite, and what kind of games, entertainment, and food you'll have. Write down as much information as you can. Later, you can decide just what you'll put into your letter.

NOTES FOR A LETTER OF INVITATION

_____

_____

_____

_____

_____

Name _____ Date _____

Party Time!
First Draft

DIRECTIONS: Write a draft in the space below for a letter of invitation. Tell about the occasion and make it seem like fun—like the sort of party you would like to attend. Address it to a real friend or a make-believe one and let that person know how much they're wanted. Include the best ideas on your brainstorming list. Use the personal letter form as directed.

_____

(Write your street address here)

_____

(Write your city, state, and zip here)

_____

(Write today's date here)

_____

Dear _____ ,

(Complete the greeting here)

_____

_____

_____

_____

_____

_____

_____

_____

_____

_____

Your friend,

(This is the closing)

_____

(Sign your name here)

© 1995 by John Wiley & Sons, Inc.

Name _____ **Date** _____

Party Time!
Revising and Writing a Final Copy

DIRECTIONS: Read the first draft of your letter of invitation. Make any changes and corrections that will make it a better letter. Follow these suggestions:

1. Is your sentence structure correct? Do the subjects and verbs agree? Correct any run-on or incomplete sentences.

2. Use a dictionary to check spelling.

3. Is the purpose of the party stated clearly? Have you used the most interesting words and phrases to make it seem fun? Did you describe some exciting activities?

4. Did you include the date, time, and place of the party?

5. Will the person receiving the letter realize how much he or she is wanted at the party?

6. Did you follow directions for correct letter form?

Write the final copy of your letter in the space below. Begin with the return address (three lines in the upper-right corner containing your address, then city, state, and zip, then date). Write the greeting (Dear _____) on the next line at the left margin. At the end of the letter, write the closing (Your friend,) on the right side, with your signature below.

_____

_____

_____

_____

_____

_____

_____

_____

_____

© 1995 by John Wiley & Sons, Inc.

Name _____ **Date** _____

Friends Across the Miles
Prewriting

Andy Fraser was surprised when the mailman delivered this letter for him.

> 25 Watkins Road
> London W2, England
> April 12, 199_
>
> Dear Andy,
>
>   Hi. My name is Scott Howard. You don't know me, but my Uncle Jim Howard met your dad last time he was in the States. Uncle Jim gave me your address because he thought it might be fun for us to be pen pals. I turned twelve last month. I have brown hair and hazel eyes. I don't like school, except for athletics. I'm on the football team. This year we've only lost two games. I love American music, especially rap. I'll tell you more about myself in my next letter if you decide to answer this one. I hope you do. You could write me all about what life is like for a kid in America, and I'll do the same from here.
>
>   Your pen pal (I hope),
>   Scott

Andy already has a pen pal. He thinks that two would be too many. So, he gave Scott's letter to you. You're going to write to Scott and offer to be his new pen pal.

BRAINSTORMING: Think about some of the things you can include in your letter. You might want to explain who you are, why you are writing, details about yourself that would be of interest to Scott, and what you'd like to know about him and his country. On the lines below, write down as many of these ideas as you can come up with. You don't have to use complete sentences—phrases will do.

BRAINSTORMING LIST

_____

_____

_____

_____

_____

© 1995 by John Wiley & Sons, Inc.

Name _____   **Date** _____

Friends Across the Miles
First Draft

DIRECTIONS: Write a draft of a letter to your new pen pal, Scott Howard. Use the notes from your brainstorming list. One way to arrange the letter is as follows: In the first paragraph, tell who you are and why you are writing. In the second paragraph, tell a little about your appearance and interests. In the third paragraph, ask a few questions about England.

_____   (Write your street address here)

_____   (City, state, zip, and USA here)

_____   (Write today's date here)

© 1995 by John Wiley & Sons, Inc.

Dear _____ , _____
(Complete the greeting here)

_____

_____

_____

_____

_____

_____

_____

_____

_____

_____

Your friend,

(This is your closing)

_____   (Sign your name here)

Name _____ Date _____

Friends Across the Miles
Revising and Writing a Final Copy

DIRECTIONS: Revise the draft of your letter to Scott Howard. Make any changes and corrections that will make it a better letter.

1. Did you explain clearly who you are and why you are writing?

2. Did you tell enough about yourself and your interests?

3. Do you express an interest in Scott and his country?

4. Is your sentence structure correct? Do subjects and verbs agree?

5. Use a dictionary to check spelling.

6. Did you follow directions for correct letter form?

Write the final copy of your letter below. Begin with the return address (three lines in the upper-right corner containing your address, then city, state, zip, and USA, then the date.) Write the greeting (Dear Scott,) on the next line at the left margin. At the end of the letter, write the closing (Your friend,) on the right side, with your signature below.

_____

_____

_____

_____

_____

_____

_____

_____

_____

_____

_____

_____

© 1995 by John Wiley & Sons, Inc.

Name _____ **Date** _____

A Buddy in Space
Prewriting

Is there intelligent life out there in space? Many scientists believe that there are life forms on other planets. Perhaps some day we'll be able to communicate with beings who live billions of miles away from us.

Let's pretend that contact has been made with aliens from a distant galaxy. They live on a planet named Astarus. They really want to get to know us, so they've started a pen pal program between Astarians and Earthlings. You've been paired up with a 12-year-old Astarian girl named Solana. It's up to you to write the first letter. First, you are going to make a list of what you might include in this letter.

DIRECTIONS: Use the brainstorming list below to make notes about what to include in your letter. In the first column, jot down information about yourself (age, description, family, friends, and hobbies). In the second column, write details about your planet and where you are located on it, such as your town, state, country, and continent. Write down as many things as you can think of that might interest Solana. You probably won't include everything in your first letter, but if you come up with a long list, you'll be able to choose the best and most exciting items.

© 1995 by John Wiley & Sons, Inc.

BRAINSTORMING LIST

ABOUT YOURSELF	*ABOUT YOUR PLANET*
_____	_____
_____	_____
_____	_____
_____	_____
_____	_____
_____	_____
_____	_____
_____	_____

Name _____ **Date** _____

A Buddy in Space
First Draft

DIRECTIONS: In the space below, write the first draft of a letter to Solana, your pen pal from the planet Astarus. Use your brainstorming list as a guide. Include the facts about yourself and your planet that would be most interesting to someone in a distant galaxy. Use the correct form for a personal letter.

_____

(Write your street address here)

_____

(Write your city, state, zip, and USA here)

_____

(Write today's date here)

_____

Dear _____ ,

(Complete the greeting here)

_____

_____

_____

_____

_____

_____

_____

_____

_____

_____

Your friend on Earth,

(This is the closing)

_____

(Sign your name here)

© 1995 by John Wiley & Sons, Inc.

Name _____ **Date** _____

A Buddy in Space
Revising and Writing a Final Copy

DIRECTIONS: Revise the draft of your letter to your Astarian pen pal, Solana. Make any changes and corrections that will make it a better, more interesting letter.

1. Do you explain clearly who you are and why you are writing?

2. Do you sound enthusiastic about having a pen pal?

3. Do you express an interest in Solana and her planet?

4. Is your sentence structure correct? Do subjects and verbs agree?

5. Use a dictionary to check spelling.

6. Did you follow directions for correct letter form?

Write the final copy of your letter below. Begin with the return address (three lines in the upper-right corner containing your address, then city, state, zip, and USA, then the date.) Write the greeting (Dear Solana,) on the next line at the left margin. At the end of the letter, write the closing on the right side, with your signature below.

© 1995 by John Wiley & Sons, Inc.

_____

_____

_____

_____

_____

_____

_____

_____

_____

_____

_____

Name _____ Date _____

Guess What I'm Doing
Prewriting

Have you ever been away from your family? Perhaps you stayed with a friend overnight, at a relative's place at the shore or mountains for a few days, or at your grandparents' house for a week. You may have gone away to camp for several weeks or even for the whole summer. Did you ever think how strange it must be for your family not to know what you are doing? Wouldn't they love to get a letter from you telling about your activities? You can practice doing it right now!

You are going to pretend that you are away from home. It can be any place you choose—one of those mentioned above or somewhere else. You can also choose anyone in your family to whom you will write. It could be your mom, your dad, your brother, your sister, or you could write to the whole family. On the first line below, tell what place you are going to be writing from. On the second line, write the name of the person to whom you will be writing.

Place: _____

Person: _____

Once you have decided where you are going to be and to whom you are going to write, get ready by compiling a brainstorming list. On the lines below, write down at least five or six activities you want to talk about. These can be things you do, things that happen to you or to others, funny or unusual situations, and so on (real or imagined). Try to think of exciting and interesting events, although you can also mention boring activities.

BRAINSTORMING LIST

_____

_____

_____

_____

_____

_____

_____

_____

© 1995 by John Wiley & Sons, Inc.

Name _____ **Date** _____

Guess What I'm Doing
First Draft

DIRECTIONS: Write a draft of a letter home from wherever you have chosen to be. You can arrange the letter clearly by dividing it into three paragraphs. Choose three of the items from your brainstorming list, one for each paragraph. In each paragraph, describe one activity or event, using exciting and interesting details. Each paragraph should have at least two sentences. Use correct personal letter form, as indicated below. (You can make up a location name and address, if you wish.)

_____
(Write street address or location name here)

_____
(City, state, and zip here)

_____
(Write today's date here)

Dear _____

(Complete the greeting here)
_____

_____

_____

_____

_____

_____

_____

_____

_____

_____

                                    Your _____ ,
_____
                              (Complete the closing here)

_____
                                (Sign your name here)

© 1995 by John Wiley & Sons, Inc.

Name _____ **Date** _____

Guess What I'm Doing
Revising and Writing a Final Copy

DIRECTIONS: Revise the draft of your letter home. Make any changes and corrections that will make it a better letter.

1. Did you describe one event or activity in each paragraph?

2. Can you add more interesting details?

3. Is your sentence structure correct? Do subjects and verbs agree?

4. Use a dictionary to check spelling.

5. Did you follow the guide for correct letter form?

Write the final copy of your letter below. Begin with the return address (three lines—the third line is today's date) in the upper-right corner. Write the greeting on the next line at the left margin (followed by a comma). At the end of the letter, write the closing on the right side, with your signature below.

_____

_____

_____

_____

_____

_____

_____

_____

_____

_____

_____

© 1995 by John Wiley & Sons, Inc.

Name _____ **Date** _____

Thanks a Lot
Prewriting

It's easy to say "thank you" when you get a present or if someone is nice to you. There are times, however, when a quick "thank you" is not enough. Perhaps the gift is very special or it's something you wanted for a long time or the person had to make an extra effort to get it for you. Maybe a friend did you a favor that kept you out of trouble or saved you from an unpleasant situation. Writing a letter as a special "thank you" is an effective way of expressing your appreciation.

Here are some possible situations:

1. You are a great fan of a particular baseball (or football, soccer, or hockey) player. Your grandmother attends a game, seeks out this athlete, and gets his or her autograph for you.

2. You arrive at school and discover that you have left your English assignment at home. Your friend gives up his lunch period to help you redo the assignment and get it in on time.

3. Your math teacher spends an hour with you after school helping you to understand a difficult problem.

4. Your sister saves all the baby-sitting money she has earned in the last three months to buy your favorite video game for your birthday.

Choose one of the above situations and write the number here _____

DIRECTIONS: Use the brainstorming list below to make notes about your letter. Write some phrases describing the event, using vivid language such as sensory words and active verbs. Use at least one simile. (For example, "I was as happy as a bear with a honeycomb.") Make up additional details about the incident and names for the people involved. The more phrases you can include on your brainstorming list, the easier it will be to write a good letter.

BRAINSTORMING LIST

_____

_____

_____

_____

© 1995 by John Wiley & Sons, Inc.

Name _____ **Date** _____

Thanks a Lot
First Draft

DIRECTIONS: Write a draft of a letter thanking someone for special help or a special gift. One way of arranging the letter is to divide it into three paragraphs. In the first paragraph, describe the incident or the gift. In the second paragraph, tell why this was so important to you. In the third paragraph, describe your feelings for this person and your appreciation. Each paragraph should have at least two sentences. Use the vivid language and similes you noted on your brainstorming list. Use correct personal letter form, as shown below.

© 1995 by John Wiley & Sons, Inc.

_____

_____ (Write your street address here)

_____ (Write your city, state, and zip here)

_____ (Write today's date here)

Dear _____ ,

(Complete the greeting here)

_____

_____

_____

_____

_____

_____

_____

_____

                                    Your _____ ,

                                    (Complete the closing here)

                                    _____

                                    (Sign your name here)

Name _____   **Date** _____

Thanks a Lot
Revising and Writing a Final Copy

DIRECTIONS: Revise the draft of your letter of special thanks. Make any changes and corrections that will make it a better letter.

1. Did you describe the incident in detail, tell how you feel about it, and express your appreciation clearly?

2. Did you use vivid language such as active verbs, sensory words, and similes to make your letter interesting?

3. Are your sentences complete? Do subjects and verbs agree?

4. Use a dictionary to check spelling.

5. Did you follow directions for correct personal letter form?

Write the final copy of your letter below. Begin with the return address (three lines in the upper-right corner containing your address, then city, state, and zip, then the date on the third line). Write the greeting on the next line at the left margin. At the end of the letter, write the closing (followed by a comma) on the right side, with your signature below.

_____

_____

_____

_____

_____

_____

_____

_____

_____

_____

_____

© 1995 by John Wiley & Sons, Inc.

Name _____ Date _____

News From Home

Prewriting

Do you have a good friend who has moved away? You probably miss that person a lot. Just imagine how hard it is for him or her to be far away from everyone and everything familiar! You have the power to bring great happiness to your friend.

A newsy letter telling all the latest happenings in your neighborhood, town, and school could go a long way toward curing homesickness. That's what you are going to do in this activity. Here are your choices:

❑ *1.* Write to a friend or acquaintance who has recently moved.

❑ *2.* Write to a friend or acquaintance who moved away a long time ago.

❑ *3.* Write to a friend or acquaintance, pretending they have moved away.

❑ *4.* Make up a name; pretend this is a friend who has recently moved.

Put a check in the box next to your choice. Then, use the brainstorming list below to list ideas for your letter.

DIRECTIONS: Make a list of recent activities that would be of interest to someone who is far away. Include news items about your neighborhood, your town, your school, your class, your teachers, your group of friends, and so on. A long list will give you a greater choice to include in the actual letter. (This list will just be a guide, so you don't have to use complete sentences. Save that for the actual letter.)

BRAINSTORMING LIST

_____

_____

_____

_____

_____

_____

_____

_____

© 1995 by John Wiley & Sons, Inc.

Name _____   Date _____

News From Home
First Draft

DIRECTIONS: You are going to make your friend (real or imaginary) incredibly happy when you share interesting news. Write a draft of your letter below. There are several ways of arranging it.

    1. Ask how your friend is getting along in the new place in the first paragraph. Use the second paragraph to relate three or four news items. Conclude in the third paragraph with ways in which that person is missed.
    2. Or you can include more paragraphs and devote each one to a particular subject (for example, one paragraph about school news, another about neighborhood news, and so on). Follow the guide for correct personal letter form below.

© 1995 by John Wiley & Sons, Inc.

_____

(Write your street address here)

_____

City, state, and zip here

_____

(Write today's date here)

_____

Dear _____ ,

(Complete the greeting here)

_____

_____

_____

_____

_____

_____

_____

         Your _____ ,

(Complete the closing here)

_____

(Sign your name here)

Name _____ Date _____

News From Home
Itemizing and Writing a Final Copy

DIRECTIONS: Revise the draft of your letter to a friend who has moved. Make any changes and corrections that will make it a better letter.

1. Did you choose the most interesting items from your brainstorming list to include in the letter?

2. Did you include different topics, such as news about friends, school, and town?

3. Did you use vivid and interesting language?

4. Are your sentences complete? Do subjects and verbs agree?

5. Did you follow directions for correct personal letter form?

Write the final copy of your letter below. Begin with the return address (three lines in the upper-right corner containing your address, then city, state, and zip, then the date on the third line.) Write the greeting on the next line at the left margin. At the end of the letter, write the closing (followed by a comma) at the right, with your signature below.

© 1995 by John Wiley & Sons, Inc.

Name _____   Date _____

Dear Owner
Prewriting

Do you have a pet? If so, you know how smart it is. If only your cat, dog, hamster, rabbit, or goldfish could speak! Even better, suppose it knew how to write letters! What would it tell you?

In this activity, you're going to imagine what a pet might say in a letter to its master. It could be your own pet or someone else's or just an imaginary one. On this worksheet, you're going to help that pet get ready to write the letter.

DIRECTIONS:

1. What kind of pet will it be? (dog, cat, and so on) _____

2. What is the pet's name? _____

3. What is the name of the pet's owner? _____

4. Describe what the pet looks like. _____

   _____

5. Prepare a brainstorming list for your pet on the lines below. List all the things you can think of that a pet might want to communicate to its owner. The more you list, the more you'll have to choose from when writing the letter.

© 1995 by John Wiley & Sons, Inc.

BRAINSTORMING LIST

_____

_____

_____

_____

_____

_____

_____

_____

Name _____ Date _____

Dear Owner
First Draft

DIRECTIONS: Can you pretend to be a cat, dog, or other pet? Try to see the world through the eyes of that creature. Here is one suggestion for arranging the letter:

1. First paragraph—Tell who you are. Introduce yourself (the pet, of course) and say why you are writing this letter.

2. Second paragraph—Choose three or four items from your brainstorming list and tell these to your owner in clear, brief sentences.

3. Third paragraph—Conclude with your opinion of your owner and how you feel about him or her.

Use correct personal letter form, as shown below.

_____

(Write the pet's street address here)

_____

(Write city, state, and zip here)

_____

(Write today's date here)

Dear _____ , _____

(Complete the greeting here)

_____

_____

_____

_____

_____

_____

Your _____ , _____

(Complete the pet's closing here)

_____

(Sign the pet's name here)

© 1995 by John Wiley & Sons, Inc.

Name _____ **Date** _____

Dear Owner
Revising and Writing a Final Copy

DIRECTIONS: Revise the draft of your pet's letter to its owner. Make changes and corrections that will make it a better letter.

1. Is the letter written through the eyes of the pet? Change any parts that seem to be from a human's viewpoint.

2. Is vivid language used to make the letter interesting? Can you find any active verbs or sensory images that will improve it?

3. Are the sentences complete? Do subjects and verbs agree?

4. Use a dictionary to correct spelling. (Pets are good spellers!)

5. Is the form correct for a personal letter?

Write the final copy of the letter below. Begin with the return address (three lines in the upper-right corner containing the pet's address, then city, state, and zip, then the date on the third line). Write the greeting at the beginning of the next line. At the end of the letter, write the closing (followed by a comma) at the right, with the pet's name below.

© 1995 by John Wiley & Sons, Inc.

_____

_____

_____

_____

_____

_____

_____

_____

_____

_____

© 1995 by John Wiley & Sons, Inc.

Name _____ Date _____

Dear Mom

Prewriting

Everybody buys cards for their moms on Mother's Day. Wouldn't you like to be different? Imagine how pleased your mom would be if, just once, you gave or mailed her a personal letter instead of an ordinary, mass-produced card.

She would love to get a long letter, expressing your love for her and telling how much you appreciate all she does for you. You could list the special things that are great about your mom, so she'll know this letter is for her and no one else. That will make her feel like a special mom indeed!

This letter will be easier to write if you first prepare a brainstorming list.

DIRECTIONS: Write a brainstorming list for a letter to your mom. Write down words and phrases that express how you feel about her. List all the different things she has done for you as well as things about your mom that make her special. Your letter will be easy to write if you include lots of details in your brainstorming list.

BRAINSTORMING LIST

_____

_____

_____

_____

_____

_____

_____

_____

_____

_____

_____

Name _____   Date _____

Dear Mom
First Draft

DIRECTIONS: Make this the best letter you have ever written! Your mom deserves that, doesn't she? Choose the best ideas from your brainstorming list, the ones you think she'll like the most. Don't be afraid to be emotional in describing your feelings. The stronger they are, the more she'll love it. Here is one suggestion for organizing the letter:

1. First paragraph—Describe how you feel about your mom. List the things that make her so special.

2. Second paragraph—Express your appreciation for all she has done for you and for the family. Tell about these things in detail.

3. Third paragraph—Tell her why you are writing this letter and mention the special occasion (Mother's Day).

Use correct personal letter form. She'll be impressed! Remember, this is just a first draft!

_____
(Write your street address here)

_____
(Write your city, state, and zip here)

_____
(Write today's date here)

Dear   ,
_____
(Complete the greeting here)

_____

_____

_____

_____

Love,
_____
(Use this or any other closing you wish)

_____
(Sign your name here)

© 1995 by John Wiley & Sons, Inc.

Name _____   **Date** _____

Dear Mom
Revising and Writing a Final Copy

DIRECTIONS: Revise the draft of your Mother's Day letter to your mom. Make changes and corrections that make it a better letter.

1. Are your words and phrases strong enough so your mom will know how important she is to you?

2. Do you include all the things that make her special? Are you sure you haven't left out something important?

3. Are the sentences complete? Do subjects and verbs agree?

4. Use a dictionary to correct spelling.

5. Is the form correct for a personal letter?

Write the final copy below. Begin with the return address (three lines at the upper-right corner containing your street address, then the city, state, and zip, then the date on the third line). Write the greeting at the beginning of the next line. At the end of the letter, write the closing (followed by a comma) halfway across the line, then your name below.

_____

_____

_____

_____

_____

_____

_____

_____

_____

_____

_____

© 1995 by John Wiley & Sons, Inc.

Name _____   Date _____

Dear Dad
Prewriting

Most of us take our fathers for granted. We don't usually tell them how much they are appreciated. Wouldn't it be nice if, just once, you told your dad what a great guy he is? Father's Day is a perfect time to do this, but you could do this any time of the year.

Most of us feel awkward sharing strong feelings face to face, even with our own parents. It's hard to do. A letter is the perfect solution. Writing a letter gives you time to think and organize your ideas so you end up with a clear expression of what you are trying to say. A brainstorming list is a good way to get ready.

DIRECTIONS: Write a brainstorming list for a letter to your dad. Write down words and phrases that express how you feel about him. List all the things he has done for you. Write down the things about your dad that make him special. The longer your brainstorming list, the easier it will be to write the letter.

BRAINSTORMING LIST

_____
_____
_____
_____
_____
_____
_____
_____
_____
_____
_____
_____

© 1995 by John Wiley & Sons, Inc.

Name _____ **Date** _____

Dear Dad
First Draft

DIRECTIONS: Your dad will be pleased to get a letter from you. Imagine how happy he'll be to read about your feelings for him and about what a wonderful father he is! Choose the best ideas from your brainstorming list. Here is one suggestion for organizing the letter:

1. First paragraph—Describe how you feel about your dad. List the things that make him special.

2. Second paragraph—Express your appreciation for all he does for you and the family. Tell about these things in detail.

3. Third paragraph—Tell him why you are writing this letter and mention the special occasion if you are doing it for Father's Day.

    Use correct personal letter form. Your dad will be impressed! Remember, this is just a first draft!

_____
                            (Write your street address here)

_____
           (Write your city, state, and zip here)

_____
                        (Write today's date here)

Dear _____ , _____
(Complete the greeting here)

_____

_____

_____

_____

_____

_____

                           Love,

_____
          (Use this or any other closing you wish)

_____
                    (Sign your name here)

© 1995 by John Wiley & Sons, Inc.

© 1995 by John Wiley & Sons, Inc.

Name _____ **Date** _____

Dear Dad

Revising and Writing a Final Copy

DIRECTIONS: Revise the draft of your letter to your dad. Make changes and corrections that will make it a better letter.

1. Have you told your dad strongly enough how you feel about him? Don't be afraid to use words and phrases like *love, admire, respect, look up to,* and *more than anyone in the world.*

2. Have you listed at least three of the most important things your father does for you and your family and explained why they are important?

3. Have you mentioned the special qualities your dad possesses that make him unique?

4. Are the sentences complete? Do subjects and verbs agree?

5. Did you use vivid language, such as active verbs and sensory images, to bring your ideas to life?

6. Is the form correct for a personal letter?

Write the final copy of the letter below. Begin with the return address (three lines in the upper-right corner containing your street address, then the city, state, and zip, then today's date). Write the greeting at the beginning of the next line. At the end of the letter, write the closing (followed by a comma) halfway across the line. Write your name below.

_____

_____

_____

_____

_____

_____

_____

_____

_____

Name _____   Date _____

Dear Twentieth-Century Folks
Prewriting

© 1995 by John Wiley & Sons, Inc.

If people from the nineteenth century were suddenly transported to our time, they would be openmouthed with astonishment. They would have no idea about most of the following: automobiles, super highways, airplanes, airports, space travel, television, audio or video cassettes, rock concerts, shopping malls, sneakers, jeans, camcorders, movie theatres, Disney World, computers, floppy disks, fax machines, microwave ovens, electricity and central heating in every home, and air conditioning. They would never have heard of professions such as computer programmer, jet pilot, fast-food worker, or disc jockey. The list could go on and on.

This has been a century of unbelievable change. The same will probably be true of the next century. What changes will occur? What new inventions and lifestyles will become common? Will they think that our way of life is primitive?

DIRECTIONS: You're going to pretend that you're a kid living in the late twenty-first century, around the year 2090. You're going to write a letter to someone stuck back in the 1990s, telling them about the wonderful (or not-so-wonderful?) new world of the future. Use your imagination to think up details about this future time. You can write about changes in countries, cities, government, family life, schools, homes, jobs, clothing styles, inventions, hobbies, vacations, and about anything else that comes into your mind. Use the brainstorming list below to jot down your ideas.

BRAINSTORMING LIST

_____

_____

_____

_____

_____

_____

_____

_____

Name _____ Date _____

Dear Twentieth-Century Folks
First Draft

DIRECTIONS: What is it like in the year 2090? The twentieth-century old-timers are eagerly waiting for your letter. Here is one way to organize it:

1. First paragraph—Tell who you are—your age, your school and classes, your family, and where you live.

2. Second paragraph—Choose four or five details from your brainstorming list. Use vivid, exciting language to describe them.

3. Third paragraph—Do you think life is better or worse in the twenty-first century? Why?

   Use correct personal letter form. Remember, this is just a first draft. Concentrate on organizing and getting down your ideas.

_____
(Write your street address here)

_____
(Write your city, state, and zip here)

_____
(Write today's date here)

Dear Twentieth-Century Folks,
_____

_____

_____

_____

_____

_____

_____

Your _____,
(Complete the closing here)

_____
(Sign your name here)

© 1995 by John Wiley & Sons, Inc.

Name _____ **Date** _____

Dear Twentieth-Century Folks
Revising and Writing a Final Copy

DIRECTIONS: Revise the draft of your letter from the twenty-first century. Make any changes and corrections that will make it a better letter.

1. Are you writing from the point of view of someone living a hundred years from now?

2. Did you use vivid, exciting language to describe details of twenty-first-century life?

3. Are your sentences complete? Do subjects and verbs agree?

4. Check spelling in a dictionary.

5. Did you follow directions for correct personal letter form?

    Write the final copy of your letter below. Begin with the return address in the upper-right corner containing your street address, city, state, and zip, then today's date). Write the greeting at the beginning of the next line. At the end of the letter, write the closing (followed by a comma) halfway across the line, with your signature below.

_____

_____

_____

_____

_____

_____

_____

_____

_____

_____

_____

_____

© 1995 by John Wiley & Sons, Inc.

UNIT SIX

Business Letters

The art of becoming an effective correspondent requires the same skills as any other sort of written expression—the ability to organize one's thoughts, to find the words that best convey them, and to structure the whole thing into a clear, coherent message. People who are comfortable with writing and have acquired the ability to use the written word effectively have no problems translating these skills into letter writing. Businesspeople, professionals, academics, and students who can write competently in any area can easily master the technical aspects of composing letters.

Younger students who have more assurance with the spoken word can be led more easily into letter writing if they can first be persuaded to see it as not very different from having a conversation. They do not usually have much difficulty learning how to write the personal letters covered in the previous unit. They sometimes encounter a block, however, when faced with the need to write something that is labeled "business" or "technical." For that reason, most of the activities in this section involve some aspect of business writing that has relevance to fourth through eighth grade students' real lives and interests, such as a letter of complaint, a letter requesting information for a school research project, and so on. Some of the final activities require more technical thinking and organization. These may pose a challenge to many students, but it is a challenge that can substantially increase their skill development in this area.

The first activity sheet illustrates and describes the correct form for a business letter. Each student should have a copy of this guide for reference when working on the subsequent activities.

Name _____ **Date** _____

Business Letter Form

Here is one correct way to set up a business letter. Other styles are sometimes used, but they all have the parts shown here.

	(Writer's street address) (City, state, and zip) (Current date) — (return address)
(inside address)	(Name of person or company to whom you are writing) (Their street address) (City, state, and zip)
(salutation)	Dear Sir or Madam (or name of person):
(body)	Your message will appear here. This is called the body of the letter. State your message clearly.
	Yours truly, (Sign your name here) — (closing)
	Enc. (This indicates that you are enclosing something with your letter.)

© 1995 by John Wiley & Sons, Inc.

1. In a business letter, the heading is called the *return address.* It is written in the upper-right corner. There are three lines in the return address. The first shows your street address. The second line indicates the city or town, state, and zip code. Use the correct post office abbreviation for the state (NJ for New Jersey, CA for California, WI for Wisconsin, and so on). Do not abbreviate the city. The date is on the third line. Do not abbreviate the month.

2. The *inside address* usually contains three lines. The first line is the name of the person or company to whom you are writing. The second line is their street address. The third line shows the city, state, and zip code. The state may be abbreviated, as described above. Each line begins at the left margin. Do not indent. (This is exactly the same as the address on the envelope.)

3. The *salutation* (or greeting) also begins at the left margin. It is followed by a comma (,) or a colon (:).

4. The *body* of the letter contains your message. You may or may not indent at the beginning of each paragraph.

5. The *closing* begins halfway across the line under the *return address*. Capitalize only the first letter of the first word. A comma (,) follows.

6. Your *signature* is written under the *closing*.

7. If you are enclosing anything with your letter, write *Enc.* at the bottom at the left margin.

8. Center your letter on the page. Use a typewriter or computer, if possible.

© 1995 by John Wiley & Sons, Inc.

© 1995 by John Wiley & Sons, Inc.

Name _____ Date _____

Can You Set Up a Business Letter?

DIRECTIONS: Answer the questions below in the space provided. All the answers can be found in Activity 81A.

1. Name one way in which a business letter is different from a personal letter. _____
_____

2. What is the first part of a business letter called? _____

3. How many lines are there in this part of the letter? _____

4. Where does this section of the letter appear? _____

5. Which line contains the date? _____

6. Name two things in this section that should not be abbreviated. _____
_____

7. Whose name and address appears in the inside address? _____
_____

8. What appears on the first line of the inside address? _____
_____

9. Where does each line of the inside address begin? _____

10. Is the salutation indented? _____

11. What punctuation marks may be used after the salutation? _____

12. What is the message part called? _____

13. Where does the closing begin? _____

14. What mark of punctuation follows the closing? _____

15. Which part of the closing is capitalized? _____

16. What does *Enc.* mean? _____

17. Where does *Enc.* appear? _____

© 1995 by John Wiley & Sons, Inc.

Name _____ **Date** _____

You've Got a Complaint!
Prewriting and First Draft

Mike Carter ordered a model airplane kit from a catalog. When it arrived, Mike was disappointed because it was incomplete and parts were broken. He wrote this letter to the mail order company.

---

95 Maple Lane
Keeswater, NJ 07000
July 2, 199_

Becker Distributors
21 Sixth Street
Providence, RI 84357

Dear Sirs:

   I am returning the Spitfire model airplane kit (Catalog Number 4958), which I ordered on June 20.

   The kit arrived yesterday in bad shape. A wing and two wheels were broken and several parts were missing.

   Please send me a kit that is in good condition or return the $3.95 that I paid for this item.

Yours truly,

Mike Carter

DIRECTIONS: You are going to pretend that you, too, ordered something from Becker Distributors about which you wish to complain. You ordered a set of four jigsaw puzzles of the United States. The box contained only three puzzles, and two of these had pieces missing. The catalog number for this item was 59045 and it cost $3.95. On a separate sheet of paper, write a first draft of your letter of complaint. Make it strong. Set it up just like the one above, as follows:

1. Put the return address in the upper-right corner, beginning about halfway across the line. (Your address on the first line, your city, state, zip on the next, and today's date on the third).

2. The name and address of the person or company to whom you are writing is called the inside address. As you can see in the letter above, it is placed on three lines, each starting at the left margin.

3. The greeting (Dear Sirs:) also begins at the left margin and is followed by a colon (:).

4. Indent at the beginning of each paragraph.

5. The closing (Yours truly,) begins at the middle of the line (lined up with the return address).

6. Your name appears below the closing.

Name _____ **Date** _____

You've Got a Complaint!
Revising and Writing a Final Copy

DIRECTIONS: Look over and correct your letter of complaint, following these suggestions:

1. Did you follow the form for a business letter, using correct placement for the return address, the inside address, the greeting, the closing, and your signature? Check your letter against the example in Activity 82A.

2. Do you clearly state the reasons for your complaint?

3. Do you indicate the catalog number and price?

4. Do you say how you want this mistake corrected?

5. Were you firm but polite?

6. Did you use correct sentence structure, with subjects and verbs agreeing, no run-on sentences, and no incomplete sentences?

7. Check your spelling in a dictionary.

Write your final copy on the lines below, using correct business letter form.

_____

_____

_____

_____

_____

_____

_____

_____

_____

_____

_____

© 1995 by John Wiley & Sons, Inc.

Name _____ **Date** _____

Get That Info!
Prewriting

Sometimes it's necessary to write a letter to get information. Matt Peterson's class was working on a unit about great inventions. Matt had to write a report on the invention of the typewriter. He looked it up in an encyclopedia and in library books. One of the books said that more information could be obtained from the Milwaukee Public Museum. Matt copied the address and wrote the following letter.

---

252 Heather Way
Rochester, NY 14618
April 3, 199_

Milwaukee Public Museum
800 West Wells Street
Milwaukee, WI 53233

Dear Sirs:

I am doing a report for my sixth-grade class on the invention of typewriters. One of the books I read said that your museum has a lot of information about this subject.

I would appreciate it if you would send me any interesting facts about this invention.

Thank you.

Yours truly,

Matt Peterson

Matt's letter did the job! The Milwaukee Museum sent him a pamphlet with many new details. His report was a big success!

DIRECTIONS: Pretend that you are assigned to write a report about one of the following:

❏ Animals of the Southwestern U.S.

❏ How Wildfires Affect Our Forests

❏ The Alligators of Florida

1. Put a check in the box next to the topic you have chosen. (You don't have to write the report, just a letter as part of your research.)

© 1995 by John Wiley & Sons, Inc.

2. You can get information on any of these subjects from the National Museum of Natural History. Here is the address: National Museum of Natural History, Washington D.C. 29560.

3. On the first line below, write a possible first sentence for your letter. On the other lines, jot down some thoughts you wish to include in your letter.

BRAINSTORMING LIST

© 1995 by John Wiley & Sons, Inc.

Name _____ **Date** _____

Get That Info!
First Draft

DIRECTIONS: Write the first draft of a letter to the National Museum of Natural History asking for information about the topic you have chosen.

1. Read Matt Peterson's letter to see how one student did this.

2. Begin the body of your letter with the sentence on your brainstorming list. The rest of the letter will be easy to write if you keep two guides handy: your brainstorming list and your sample business letter (Activity 81A).

3. Be sure you correctly place the return address and date, the inside address, the salutation, the body, the closing, and your signature. (In this letter, the inside address will have only two lines.)

Write your first draft on the lines below. Remember, this is only a draft!

_____
(Write your street address here)

_____
(Your city, state, and zip here)

_____
(Write today's date here)

National Museum of Natural History

Washington, DC 29560

_____

_____ : _____

(Write the salutation here)

[Begin the body (message) here]

_____

_____

_____

_____ , __

(Write the closing here)

_____
(Sign your name here)

© 1995 by John Wiley & Sons, Inc.

Name _____ **Date** _____

Get That Info!
Revising and Writing a Final Copy

DIRECTIONS: Revise the draft of your letter requesting information from the National Museum of Natural History. Make any changes and corrections that will make it a better letter. Here are some things to look for:

1. Does the beginning of your letter say who you are and why you are writing?

2. Do you state exactly what information you want?

3. Is your letter polite and clearly written?

4. Are your sentences complete? Do subjects and verbs agree?

5. Is there any spelling you're not sure about? Consult a dictionary.

6. Compare your letter carefully with the sample of a business letter. Did you use correct business letter form?

Write the final copy of your letter below.

_____

_____

_____

_____

_____

_____

_____

_____

_____

_____

_____

_____

© 1995 by John Wiley & Sons, Inc.

Name _____ Date _____

Let's Shop!
Prewriting

It's fun to shop by mail. Before you can do it, however, you must have a catalog.

Jeni Brown takes ballet lessons. In her dance studio, she noticed a catalog of dance supplies. She wanted to get a copy of this catalog for herself, so she copied the address and wrote the following letter.

© 1995 by John Wiley & Sons, Inc.

243 Allan Street
Richmond, VA 23228
October 3, 199_

Lee Dance Supplies
P.O. Box 355
Los Angeles, CA 90069

Dear Sirs:

Please put my name on your mailing list and send me a copy of your latest catalog. I am interested in ordering leotards and slippers.
Thank you.

Yours truly,

Jeni Brown

It's fun to receive catalogs. In this activity, you are going to practice sending away for one, using correct business letter form.

DIRECTIONS:

1. Choose one of the following catalog companies:

Global Computer Supplies   (Computer supplies)
11 Harbor Park Drive
Port Washington, NY 10050

L.L. Bean, Inc.   (Outdoor and camping
Freeport, ME 04033   clothing and supplies)

Miles Kimball   (Small general items, such
41 West Eighth Ave.   as toys, household gadgets,
Oshkosh, WI 54906   holiday items, etc.)

2. Use the brainstorming list below to get ready to write your letter. On the first line, write the name of the catalog company you have chosen. On the second line, write a beginning sentence. Under that, list some of the thoughts you want to include in your letter. (You might wish to mention the kind of items that especially interest you.)

BRAINSTORMING LIST

© 1995 by John Wiley & Sons, Inc.

© 1995 by John Wiley & Sons, Inc.

Name _____ Date _____

Let's Shop!
First Draft

© 1995 by John Wiley & Sons, Inc.

DIRECTIONS: Write the first draft of a letter to the catalog company you have chosen.

1. Read Jeni Brown's letter. Use it as a guide, together with your brainstorming list and your sample business letter (Activity 81A).
2. Begin with the sentence you prepared for the brainstorming list.
3. Mention the kind of items you are interested in ordering.
4. Be sure you correctly place the return address (including date), the inside address, the salutation, the body, the closing, and your name.

Write your first draft on the lines below. Remember, this is only a draft!

_____
(Write your street address here)

_____
(Your city, state, and zip here)

_____
(Write today's date here)

(Name of company here)
_____

(Company's street address or box # here)
_____

(Their city, state, and zip here)
_____
:

(Write the salutation here)
_____

(Begin the body [message] here)
_____

_____

_____

_____

_____

_____ , _____

(Write the closing here)

_____
(Sign your name here)

205

Name _____   Date _____

Let's Shop!
Revising and Writing a Final Copy

DIRECTIONS: Revise the draft of your letter asking for a catalog. Make any changes and corrections that will make it a better letter. Here are some things to look for:

1. Does the beginning of your letter state your reason for writing?

2. Do you mention the particular kind of items in which you are interested?

3. Is your letter polite and clearly written?

4. Are your sentences complete? Do subjects and verbs agree?

5. Consult a dictionary for spelling.

6. Compare your letter carefully with the sample of a business letter. Is the form correct?

Write the final copy of your letter below.

_____

_____

_____

_____

_____

_____

_____

_____

_____

_____

_____

_____

_____

© 1995 by John Wiley & Sons, Inc.

Name _____   **Date** _____

It's Our World, Too!
Prewriting

There is a county park at one end of town. It has acres of woods, a playground, and a pond. The kids in town love it. So do the grownups. Now, the county may sell the park. A developer wants to cut down the woods, dam the pond, and build a shopping center. Some people have formed a Save-Our-Park Committee. They have written letters to the county planning board telling how much the park means to them. Here is one such letter:

© 1995 by John Wiley & Sons, Inc.

> 243 Garden Place
> Colby, OH 45067
> March 20, 199_
>
> Planning Board
> Colby County Courthouse
> Colby, OH 45067
>
> Dear Planning Board:
>
> There used to be a lot of undeveloped land and many parks in Colby County. Most of it is now the site of shopping malls and housing developments. All that's left is Colby Park.
>
> This park is needed in Colby County. Our children want a place to play that isn't concrete and metal. We all need the woods and greenery to purify the air we breathe.
>
> Please don't sell off what little remains of our natural resources. Let's preserve Colby County Park for our children and grandchildren.
>
> Yours truly,
>
> Arthur Ransome

DIRECTIONS: The Save-Our-Park Committee has asked kids to write to the Planning Board, too. Use the brainstorming list below to make notes for your letter to the Planning Board. You can include some of the same points as the letter above. Add others from a kid's point of view, such as what you do in the park (playing ball, enjoying the woods and birds, picnicking, fishing in the pond, using the playground, and so on). How would Colby County be different without the park? Write a beginning sentence for your letter on the first line. Below it, list the points you want to make in your letter.

BRAINSTORMING LIST

_____

_____

_____

_____

Name _____   **Date** _____

It's Our World, Too!
First Draft

DIRECTIONS: Write the first draft of a letter to the Planning Board of Colby County asking them to preserve the park.

1. Read Arthur Ransome's letter. Use it as a guide, together with your brainstorming list and your sample business letter (Activity 81A).

2. Begin your letter with the first sentence you prepared for the brainstorming list.

3. Include some of Mr. Ransome's facts. Add at least three more things from a kid's point of view that make it important to keep the park.

4. Be sure you correctly place the return address (including date), the inside address (same as in Mr. Ransome's letter), the salutation, the body, the closing, and your name.

Write your first draft below. Remember, this is only a draft!

_____

(Write your street address here)

_____

(Write your city, state, and zip here)

_____

(Write today's date here)

(Write *Planning Board* here)
_____

(Write *Colby County Courthouse* here)
_____

(Write *Colby, OH 45067* here)   :
_____

(Write the salutation here)
_____

(Begin the body [message] here)
_____

_____

_____

_____

                                                                ,
_____

(Write the closing here)
_____

(Sign your name here)

© 1995 by John Wiley & Sons, Inc.

Name _____   **Date** _____

It's Our World, Too!
Revising and Writing a Final Copy

DIRECTIONS: Revise the draft of your letter to the Planning Board. Make any changes and corrections that will make it a better letter. Here are some things to look for:

1. Does the beginning of your letter state your reason for writing?

2. Are your points logical and clearly stated? Do you emphasize how important this park is to you? Can you phrase any of your ideas more strongly?

3. Can you think of anything else to say that might convince the Planning Board to preserve your park?

4. Are your sentences complete? Do subjects and verbs agree?

5. Is all spelling correct? Consult a dictionary.

6. Compare your letter with the sample of a business letter. Is the form correct?

   Write the final copy of your letter below.

_____

_____

_____

_____

_____

_____

_____

_____

_____

_____

_____

_____

© 1995 by John Wiley & Sons, Inc.

Name _____   Date _____

I Can Help
Prewriting

Wouldn't you like to do something for someone else? It can be very satisfying to help others.

There is an article in your local newspaper that says volunteers are needed in hospitals, senior citizen homes, day-care centers, and other places. The article states that even kids your age can help. You are going to write a letter offering to be a volunteer. Here is an example:

309 Bridge Street
Middletown, RI 08457
June 4, 199_

Mr. William Pfeiffer, Volunteer Coordinator
2 State Street
Middletown, RI 08457

Dear Mr. Pfeiffer:

I would like to do volunteer work. I am 12 years old, in the seventh grade at Central Middle School. I get a lot of homework and also have a daily paper route, but I could give five or six hours a week as a volunteer.

I would be willing to work wherever needed. I am athletic and could help little kids with sports. I am also good at reading aloud. I'd like to read to little kids or to old people with bad eyesight. I am honest and reliable.

I hope you can use me as a volunteer.

Yours truly,

Jesse Moran

© 1995 by John Wiley & Sons, Inc.

DIRECTIONS: You are going to write a letter offering to be a volunteer. Use the brainstorming list below to get ready.

1. Write a first sentence for your letter on the first line. This beginning should state why you are writing.

2. Below that, make notes for your letter. Write down things you are good at that might be useful in volunteer work. Mention several kinds of work or things you can do. List your reasons for wanting to volunteer.

BRAINSTORMING LIST

_____

_____

_____

Name _____ **Date** _____

I Can Help
First Draft

DIRECTIONS: Write the first draft of a letter offering to be a volunteer in your community. Here are some suggestions.

1. Read Jesse Moran's letter. Use it as a guide, together with your brainstorming list and your sample business letter (Activity 81A).

2. Use the same inside address and greeting as in Jesse's letter.

3. Begin your letter with the first sentence you prepared for the brainstorming list.

4. Describe yourself—your age, interests, and special abilities. Use the items in your brainstorming list. Tell why you want to be a volunteer and what sort of work you'd prefer.

5. Be sure you correctly place the return address (including the date), the inside address, the salutation, the body, the closing, and your name.

Write your first draft below. Remember, this is only a draft!

_____

(Write your street address here)

_____

(Write your city, state, and zip here)

_____

(Write today's date here)

(Copy first line of inside address from Jesse's letter here)

(Copy second line of inside address here)

(Copy third line of inside address here)
:

(Copy salutation here)

(Begin the body [message] here)

_____

_____

_____

_____ ,

(Write the closing here)

_____

(Sign your name here)

© 1995 by John Wiley & Sons, Inc.

Name _____   **Date** _____

I Can Help
Revising and Writing a Final Copy

DIRECTIONS: Revise the draft of your letter offering to work as a volunteer. Make any changes and corrections that will make it a better letter. Here are some things to look for:

1. Does the beginning of your letter state your reason for writing?

2. Do you give enough information about yourself? Have you left out any interests or special abilities that might be useful as a volunteer?

3. Is the tone of your letter polite, enthusiastic, and positive?

4. Are your sentences complete? Do subjects and verbs agree?

5. Is the spelling correct? Consult a dictionary.

6. Compare your letter with the sample of a business letter. Is the form correct?

Write the final copy of your letter below.

_____

_____

_____

_____

_____

_____

_____

_____

_____

_____

_____

_____

_____

© 1995 by John Wiley & Sons, Inc.

Name _____   **Date** _____

Dear Box Number

Prewriting

Do you ever look at classified ads? Some of the listings you might find are *Lost and Found, Merchandise for Sale, Employment, Musical Instruments, Pets,* and others. Here's an ad that might interest you:

> *FREE TO GOOD HOME. Calico kittens, 6 weeks old, 3 males, 1 female. Box #45, Middletown Gazette, Middletown, VT 78567*

You want one of these kittens. Since there is no phone number in the ad, you'll have to write a letter. Here is an example:

---

56 Post Hill Rd.
Middletown, VT 78567
October 3, 199_

Box #45
Middletown Gazette
Middletown, VT 78567

Dear Box #45:

    My name is Erica Greco, and I would like to have one of your kittens. All my life I've wanted a calico cat, but I couldn't have one in our small apartment. Now we live in a big old farmhouse on five acres, and my parents say that I can have that calico. They like cats, too.
    Can I come and see your kittens? I know they'll like me because they'll be able to see how much I love them. Either a male or female would be fine with me. Please write or call me at 789-0001. Thanks.

Yours truly,

Erica Greco

DIRECTIONS: Use the brainstorming list on the next page to make notes for a letter answering the classified ad above. (If you would rather find a real classified ad to answer in your local newspaper, you may do so.)

1. On the first line, write a beginning sentence in which you clearly state why you are writing.

2. On the lines that follow, list some of the points you could make in your letter. You can tell about yourself, your family, any other pets past or present, why you want this kitten, why it would be happy in your home, and whether there is other information you need about it.

© 1995 by John Wiley & Sons, Inc.

BRAINSTORMING LIST

© 1995 by John Wiley & Sons, Inc.

Name _____ **Date** _____

Dear Box Number
First Draft

DIRECTIONS: Write the first draft of a reply to the classified ad about calico kittens. (Or you can choose a different ad.)

1. Read Erica Greco's letter. Use it as a guide, together with your brainstorming list and your sample business letter (Activity 81A).

2. Use the box number and newspaper address for your inside address.

3. Use the first sentence you prepared for the brainstorming list.

4. Use the items on your brainstorming list to help you explain why you want a calico cat and to describe yourself, your family, and your home.

5. Use correct business letter form for the return address (including date), the inside address, the salutation, the body, the closing, and your name.

Write your first draft below. Remember, this is only a draft!

_____
(Write your street address here)
_____
(Write your city, state, and zip here)
_____
(Write today's date here)
_____
(Write the box number here)
_____
(Write their name of the newspaper here)
_____
(Write their city, state, and zip here)
      :
_____
(Write the salutation here)
_____
(Begin the body [message] here)
_____

_____

_____

_____ ,
_____
(Write the closing here)
_____
(Sign your name here)

© 1995 by John Wiley & Sons, Inc.

Dear Box Number
Revising and Writing a Final Copy

DIRECTIONS: Revise the draft of your letter answering a classified ad. Make any changes and corrections that will make it a better letter. Here are some things to look for:

1. Does your first sentence state your reason for writing?

2. Do you give enough information about yourself and your family to convince the owner that your home would be a good one for the cat? Can you think of anything to add?

3. Are your sentences complete? Do subjects and verbs agree?

4. Is the spelling correct? Consult a dictionary.

5. Compare your letter with the sample of a business letter. Is the form correct?

Write the final copy of your letter below.

_____

_____

_____

_____

_____

_____

_____

_____

_____

_____

_____

_____

_____

© 1995 by John Wiley & Sons, Inc.

Name _____   **Date** _____

Team Business Manager
Prewriting

Heather Coleman is the business manager for her softball team. When the team needed new caps, she wrote the following letter:

---

                                                    24 Columbus Pl.
                                                    St. Petersburg, FL 33702
                                                    September 24, 199_

Active Sports Supply Co.
P.O. Box 401
Los Angeles, CA 90065

Dear Sirs:

    I would like to order 20 new caps for my team, the Sumner School Saints. We want the blue and white caps, #3591 in your fall catalog, at a price of $5.98 each. We would like to have the letter "S" printed on each cap, as shown in your catalog for $1.00 more per cap.

    Please ship this order as soon as possible, and send the bill to me at the above address. Thank you.

                                                    Yours truly,

                                                    Heather Coleman

---

The team thought the caps were awesome. Now they need new uniforms, but Heather is no longer business manager. You are! You will have to write a letter to the Active Sports Supply Company.

DIRECTIONS: The uniform the team has chosen is on page 2 of the spring 1995 catalog, catalog #3240. It comes in the following colors: black and white, blue and white, and red and white. The sizes available are small, medium, and large. The price is $24.98 each. There is an extra charge for special lettering. It costs $1.00 extra per shirt for small letters, and $2.00 for large print. Your team wants the name SAINTS printed on the back of each.

    You will have to make the following decisions: number of uniforms needed, color, sizes, and type of lettering. Use the brainstorming list on the next page to write down your choices. Also, list all the other information you will need to include in the letter. On the last line, write a first sentence for your letter.

© 1995 by John Wiley & Sons, Inc.

BRAINSTORMING LIST

© 1995 by John Wiley & Sons, Inc.

Name _____ **Date** _____

Team Business Manager
First Draft

DIRECTIONS: Write the first draft of a letter as business manager of your team, ordering uniforms.

1. Read Heather's letter. Use it as a guide, together with your Brainstorming List and your sample business letter (Activity 81A).

2. Use the same inside address as in Heather's letter.

3. Begin your letter with the first sentence you prepared for your brainstorming list.

4. Be sure you include all the information the company will need to deliver the right uniforms.

5. Use correct placement for all parts of this business letter, as shown in your sample.

Write your first draft below. Remember, this is only a draft!

_____

_____
(Write your street address here)

_____
(Write your city, state, and zip here)

_____
(Write today's date here)

_____
(Write name of catalog company here)

_____
(Write the P.O. box number here)

_____
(Write their city, state, and zip here)

_____ :
(Write the salutation here)

_____
(Begin the body [message] here)

_____

_____

_____

_____

_____

_____ ,
(Write the closing here)

_____
(Sign your name here)

© 1995 by John Wiley & Sons, Inc.

Name _____ **Date** _____

Team Business Manager
Revising and Writing a Final Copy

DIRECTIONS: Revise the draft of your letter ordering uniforms for your team. Make any changes and corrections that will make it a better letter. Here are some things to look for:

1. Does the beginning of your letter state your reason for writing?

2. Do you give all the information needed to fill your order properly? Are you sure you didn't leave anything out?

3. Are your sentences complete? Do subjects and verbs agree?

4. Use a dictionary to check spelling.

5. Compare your letter with the business letter sample. Is the form correct?

Write the final copy of your letter below.

_____

_____

_____

_____

_____

_____

_____

_____

_____

_____

_____

_____

_____

© 1995 by John Wiley & Sons, Inc.

Name _____   **Date** _____

Dear Editor
Prewriting

A newspaper editorial expresses the editor's opinion about a particular subject. A recent editorial in a school newspaper, *The Roosevelt Reporter*, suggested that the school should sponsor a gymnastics team just as it does for other sports, such as softball or soccer.

Matt Browning disagrees. He wrote this letter to the editor:

© 1995 by John Wiley & Sons, Inc.

---

975 Miller Street
Middletown, CT 06457
November 2, 199_

Editor, *The Roosevelt Reporter*
Roosevelt Middle School
Middletown, CT 06457

Dear Editor:

I am in sixth grade at Roosevelt Middle School, and I disagree with the editorial in the October issue of the *Reporter*.

I don't think we need a gymnastics team. We already have too many teams—soccer, softball, basketball, and wrestling. It's hard to make a choice. Besides, we can't have teams for every single sport. Should there be a bicycling team, a volleyball team, a tennis team, a golf team? I don't think so.

Yours truly,

Matt Browning

Matt's letter was printed on the "Letters To The Editor" page in the November issue of the *Reporter*. This is where readers can express their ideas. Who's right about the gymnastics team—the editor or Matt? You're going to write a letter to the editor telling what you think.

First, organize your thoughts with a brainstorming list. Follow the directions on the brainstorming list below.

BRAINSTORMING LIST

Write a first sentence for your letter, telling who you are. _____

_____

Write a sentence stating the topic you are writing about and whether you agree or disagree with the editorial. _____

_____

On the lines below, write down at least three reasons for your opinion. (No sentences—just words or phrases.)

1. _____   3. _____

2. _____   4. _____

© 1995 by John Wiley & Sons, Inc.

© 1995 by John Wiley & Sons, Inc.

Name _____   Date _____

Dear Editor
First Draft

DIRECTIONS: Write the first draft of a letter to the editor of *The Roosevelt Reporter*.

1. Examine Matt Browning's letter. Use it as a guide, together with your brainstorming list and your sample business letter (Activity 81A).

2. Use the same inside address as in Matt's letter.

3. Begin your letter with the first sentence you prepared for your brainstorming list. Follow that with your sentence that states the topic and expresses your opinion. This will be your first paragraph.

4. State three reasons for your opinion. This will be a second paragraph. Be clear and convincing.

5. Use correct business letter form, as in your sample letter.

Write your first draft below. Remember, this is only a draft!

_____

(Write your street address here)

_____

(Write your city, state, and zip here)

_____

(Write today's date here)

(Write Editor and name of newspaper here)

_____

(Write school name here)

_____

(Write city, state, and zip here)

:

_____

(Write salutation here)

_____

(Begin the body [message] here)

_____

_____

,

_____

(Write the closing here)

_____

(Sign your name here)

Name _____ **Date** _____

Dear Editor
Revising and Writing a Final Copy

DIRECTIONS: Revise the draft of your letter to the editor. Make any changes and corrections that will make it a better letter.

1. Does your first paragraph tell who you are, the topic you are writing about, and your opinion?

2. Does the second paragraph state at least three reasons for your opinion? Is it clear and convincing?

3. Are your sentences complete? Do subjects and verbs agree?

4. Check spelling in a dictionary.

5. Are the parts of your business letter placed correctly? Check with the sample letter.

    Write the final copy of your letter below.

_____

_____

_____

_____

_____

_____

_____

_____

_____

_____

_____

_____

© 1995 by John Wiley & Sons, Inc.

Name _____   Date _____

Radio Station Rock 106
Prewriting

Words have power! You can make things happen with letters. For example, radio stations want to satisfy their listeners. They pay attention to letters from the fans.

Radio station Rock, 106 has just fired one of their deejays, Big Andy Ames. He is your favorite deejay and you always listen to his program. If the station manager gets enough letters from angry fans, he'll probably bring Big Andy back. Here is the kind of letter you could write:

© 1995 by John Wiley & Sons, Inc.

---

25 Acton Way
Elmwood, IN 47306
July 20, 199_

Station Manager, Rock 106
201 Main Street
Elmwood, IN 47306

Dear Sir:

I can't believe that Big Andy Ames is gone! He was great!

I am 13 years old, in the seventh grade at Elmwood Junior High School. All my classmates agree with me that Big Andy was the best deejay on the air. He was funny and played the music kids enjoy. There's no reason to turn the dial to 106 unless Big Andy is there.

Bring Big Andy back!

Andy's #1 fan,

Sean Gabriel

One letter isn't going to do the job. All of Big Andy's fans should write to the station. That means you! The brainstorming list on the next page will help you prepare to write your letter.

DIRECTIONS: On the first line of the brainstorming list, write a first sentence for your letter. Make it strong enough to grab the station manager's attention.

On the lines that follow, list the other facts you want to include in your letter, such as something about yourself and all the reasons why Big Andy should get his job back.

BRAINSTORMING LIST

© 1995 by John Wiley & Sons, Inc.

Name _____ **Date** _____

Radio Station Rock 106
First Draft

DIRECTIONS: Write the first draft of a letter to radio station Rock 106 protesting the firing of Big Andy Ames.

1. Examine Sean Gabriel's letter. Use it as a guide, together with your brainstorming list and your sample business letter (Activity 81A).

2. Use the same inside address as Sean's letter.

3. Begin your letter with the first sentence you prepared for the brainstorming list. Follow that with a sentence about yourself and why you are writing this letter. This is your first paragraph.

4. In the second paragraph, state how you feel about Big Andy and your reasons for wanting him back, as listed on your brainstorming list.

5. Finish with a strong statement that will persuade the station manager to put Big Andy back on the air.

6. Use correct business letter form, as in your sample letter.

Write your first draft below. Remember, this is only a draft!

_____

(Write your street address here)

_____

(Write your city, state, and zip here)

_____

(Write today's date here)

_____

(Write Station Manager and name of station here)

_____

(Write street address here)

_____

(Write city, state, and zip here)

_____

(Write salutation here)

_____

(Begin the body [message] here)

_____

_____

_____

(Write the closing here)

_____

(Sign your name here)

© 1995 by John Wiley & Sons, Inc.

Name _____ **Date** _____

Radio Station Rock 106
Revising and Writing a Final Copy

DIRECTIONS: Revise the draft of your letter to radio station Rock 106. Make any changes and corrections to make it a better letter.

1. Do you begin with a strong statement to grab attention? Do you complete the first paragraph by telling something about yourself and why you are writing?

2. Does the next paragraph clearly tell how you feel about Big Andy's program and why you think it is good?

3. Is your final statement strong and convincing?

4. Are your sentences complete? Do subjects and verbs agree?

5. Use a dictionary to check spelling.

6. Are the parts of a business letter placed correctly?

Write the final copy of your letter below.

_____

_____

_____

_____

_____

_____

_____

_____

_____

_____

_____

_____

_____

© 1995 by John Wiley & Sons, Inc.

Name _____ Date _____

© 1995 by John Wiley & Sons, Inc.

Summer Cash
Prewriting

A summer job can be fun! It's a good way to earn money and get work experience at the same time. Here are three ads from a local newspaper, *The Felton Gazette*, in Felton, NJ 07403:

Mother's helper wanted to live with local family at beach home for summer. Light housework. Help care for adorable three-year-old twins. Write giving age, experience and salary. Box #96.

Junior counselors and counselors-in-training at nearby day camp. Swimming, music, arts & crafts, sports. State age and qualifications. Box #73

Garage mechanic's helper. Will train. Full-time summer. Possible part-time later. Box #50

Pat Connors wrote the following letter:

---

35 Bower Road
Felton, NJ 07403
May 2, 199_

Box #73
The Felton Gazette
Felton, NJ 07403

Dear Sirs:

I would like to apply for a job as counselor-in-training.

I have attended Camp Kahwanee for the past four summers, where I excelled at swimming and sports, especially softball and tennis. Last year, I won the award for best all-around athlete.

I want to be a counselor this summer so I can help younger kids have fun and improve their skills. Mr. Alan Kramer, the director of Camp Kahwanee, said that he would give me a reference.

Yours truly,

Pat Connors

DIRECTIONS: Choose one of the three job offerings above. Prepare a brainstorming list to help prepare for your letter of application. Write a beginning sentence on the first line. (This first sentence should tell why you are writing the letter.) Under that, list any skills or qualities you have that would help in that job.

BRAINSTORMING LIST

_____

_____

_____

_____

_____

_____

_____

_____

_____

_____

_____

_____

_____

_____

_____

_____

_____

_____

_____

_____

_____

_____

© 1995 by John Wiley & Sons, Inc.

Name _____ **Date** _____

Summer Cash
First Draft

DIRECTIONS: Write the first draft of a letter applying for one of the three jobs listed in Activity 91A.

1. Read Pat Connors's letter. Use it as a guide, together with your brainstorming list and your sample business letter (Activity 81A).

2. Use the box number at the end of the ad. The rest of the inside address is the same as the one in Pat's letter.

3. Begin your letter with the sentence you wrote in your brainstorming list. Your second paragraph should include the qualifications on your list. In the third paragraph, give a convincing reason why you should get the job.

4. Use correct business letter form, as in your sample letter.

Write your first draft below.

_____

_____
(Write your street address here)

_____
(Write your city, state, and zip here)

_____
(Write today's date here)

_____
(Write the Box # here)

_____
(Write the name of the newspaper here)

_____
(Write the city, state, and zip here)

_____ : _____
(Write salutation here)

_____
(Begin the body [message] here)

_____

_____

_____

_____

_____ , _____
(Write the closing here)

_____
(Sign your name here)

© 1995 by John Wiley & Sons, Inc.

Name _____ **Date** _____

Summer Cash
Revising and Writing a Final Copy

DIRECTIONS: Revise the draft of your letter applying for a summer job. Make any changes and corrections that will make it a better letter.

1. Does the first paragraph tell why you are writing?

2. Does the second paragraph clearly state your skills and personal qualifications that fit this particular job?

3. Does the third paragraph give a convincing reason why you should get this job?

4. Are your sentences complete? Do subjects and verbs agree?

5. Check spelling in a dictionary.

6. Are the parts of the letter correctly placed? Compare with your sample business letter.

Write the final copy of your letter below.

_____

_____

_____

_____

_____

_____

_____

_____

_____

_____

_____

_____

© 1995 by John Wiley & Sons, Inc.

Name _____   **Date** _____

Follow the Leader
Prewriting

Have you ever tried to show someone how to operate a machine or put something together? It's easy when you can demonstrate what you are doing. It's harder when the person is not there and you must give the directions in writing. Companies that make or sell products often have to do this for their customers. Can you describe the steps of such a process in a letter? That's what you'll learn to do in this activity.

DIRECTIONS: Choose one of the following to describe. Check the box next to your choice.

❑ *1.* How to operate a computer

❑ *2.* How to play a board game (Monopoly®, chess, Scrabble®)

❑ *3.* How to play football, baseball, or another team sport

❑ *4.* How to bake a cake or prepare a meal

❑ *5.* How to drive a car

On the brainstorming list below, list each step that must be followed. Try to list the steps in order. Don't leave out anything that the reader must know in order to do the procedure successfully.

BRAINSTORMING LIST

_____

_____

_____

_____

_____

_____

_____

_____

_____

© 1995 by John Wiley & Sons, Inc.

Name _____ **Date** _____

Follow the Leader
First Draft

DIRECTIONS: Write the first draft of a letter explaining the procedure you have chosen. Address your letter to any friend or relative (inside address). Use your sample business letter (Activity 81A) as a guide.

1. In the first paragraph, state the reason for writing and tell how you came to know so much about the subject.

2. In the second paragraph, describe the process. Take the steps as listed on your brainstorming list and put them into sentence form. Be sure to include every step. Don't leave out anything.

3. Finish your letter in the last paragraph by telling something interesting about your subject, such as how it can be useful or fun.

Write your first draft below.

_____
(Write your street address here)

_____
(Write your city, state, and zip here)

_____
(Write today's date here)

_____
(Write your friend's or relative's name here)

_____
(Write his or her street address here)

_____
(Write the city, state, and zip here)
                                    :
_____
(Write the salutation here)

_____
(Begin the body [message] here)

_____

_____

_____

_____

_____
(Write the closing here)

_____
(Sign your name here)

© 1995 by John Wiley & Sons, Inc.

Name _____   **Date** _____

Follow the Leader
Revising and Writing a Final Copy

DIRECTIONS: Revise the draft of your letter explaining how to use an item or play a game. Improve it with changes and corrections.

1. Does the first paragraph clearly state why you are writing and how you know the subject so well?

2. Does the second paragraph outline the necessary steps? Are the directions stated clearly in a logical order? Is there any additional information that may be needed?

3. Does the third paragraph sum up why it is a good thing to know how to do this?

4. Are the parts of a business letter placed correctly?

Write the final copy of your letter below.

_____

_____

_____

_____

_____

_____

_____

_____

_____

_____

_____

_____

_____

_____

© 1995 by John Wiley & Sons, Inc.

UNIT SEVEN

Creative Writing

Creative writing activities serve several important purposes in any writing program. First, they can make the writing process more meaningful by tapping into students' individual interests, fears, joys, sense of humor, and aspirations. Most kids enjoy creative writing and are, therefore, more inclined to willingly accept the steps of the writing process and adapt these to their own needs. These projects also nurture creativity and encourage students to become comfortable with writing as a vehicle for self-expression and original thinking.

Two additional factors are necessary for real success in this area. The activities themselves have to appeal to the students, and the teacher's attitude toward them must be upbeat and enthusiastic. Many of the activities in this unit were tested in the author's own writing workshops for young people with overwhelmingly positive results. The activities have been designed with a student-centered approach and from a kid's point of view. Nevertheless, worksheets, no matter how well-thought-out and attractively-designed, have their limitations. A presentation by the teacher that creates a sense of excitement and purpose will go a long way toward inspiring the students to respond in kind and put forth their best efforts. The results, in terms of exciting, original work, can be amazing.

Most of the writing activities in this unit utilize three worksheets, one for each step of the writing process (prewriting, writing a first draft, and revising and writing a final copy), although some that are designed to encourage an uninhibited flow of writing may omit the prewriting portion. This does not mean that student writing should be restricted or narrowed to fit a certain format. Students should be encouraged to be spontaneous and original, especially when performing prewriting activities or writing a first draft. Even in the final copy, originality should not be discouraged, only modified where carelessness with language and structure fails to achieve the student's own goals.

One of the biggest problems young writers have with creative writing is their inability to recognize such failures. They know how they feel and what they want to communicate and assume that the reader will also know this. Getting them to recognize when this does not happen will help them take giant steps toward becoming competent writers. Small-group critiquing is enormously helpful in accomplishing this. Spotting the flaws in the work of others not only helps the writer of that particular story, but makes the reader-critic better able to improve his or her own efforts. Small-group critiquing is specifically suggested for some of the activities in this unit, but it can be used throughout with positive results. It can be effective to form these small groups at the beginning of a creative writing unit and keep the same groups throughout. This may encourage a sense of familiarity and trust, and make it easier for students to share and critique with comfort and honesty.

The teacher will have to determine which worksheets best suit specific grade levels and abilities, but all the activities can be used for any group in grades four through eight. The responses and results will vary according to grade level, maturity, and writing ability.

The primary purpose of the activities in this unit is to guide students in using language that is not only creative and imaginative, but also effectively communicates their thoughts, feelings, and ideas.

Name _____ Date _____

Getting Ideas
First Draft and Group Sharing

It's fun to write stories or imaginative essays. The hardest part is just getting started. Some people have trouble coming up with ideas. Do you have that problem? It really isn't difficult if you know how to go about it.

You don't have to be a "born writer" to have fun with imaginative writing. This activity will show you how easy it can be to get ideas. It will also get you started simply and without pain.

Here is the beginning of a story:

> Jason got home from school at about 3:30 P.M. Something was different. His mom's blue Honda was not in the driveway. The basketball hoop was gone. Puzzled, Jason ran up to the front door. Stranger and stranger! The door had been white when he had left that morning. Now it was green. Worst of all, the nameplate now read, "Collins." That was not his name!

DIRECTIONS: Continue this story on the lines below. Use your own imagination to decide what could happen. Where could Jason's family be? What has happened when he goes inside? Who could be there? What might Jason do? You don't have to finish the story; just write for 15 minutes. (Use the back of the paper if you need more room.)

_____

_____

_____

_____

_____

_____

GROUP SHARING: Meet with your small group and share your stories. You may be surprised to see how different they all are. Try to give helpful suggestions, such as:

1. Is there anything that is not clear that the author must explain in more detail?

2. Is there anything that doesn't make sense?

3. Can you think of any ways to improve the language with different words and phrases?

4. Would the story be more effective with a word, phrase, or sentence cut?

Write down the suggestions that are made for your own story.

© 1995 by John Wiley & Sons, Inc.

Name _____   **Date** _____

Getting Ideas
Revising and Writing a Final Copy

DIRECTIONS: Revise your story about Jason and his strange homecoming. First, consider all the suggestions made by your group. If you agree that these will improve your story, make the changes on your copy. Here are some more suggestions:

1. Does your story follow logically from the beginning?

2. Does Jason act the way a real kid would?

3. Do you show his thoughts and feelings clearly?

4. Are other characters clearly described?

5. Do you always use the most effective word or phrase? Are there some that can be improved?

6. Are your sentences complete? Do subjects and verbs agree?

When your story is as good as you can make it, write the final copy below. Be sure to include the beginning that is on Activity 93A. (Use the back of this paper if you need more room.)

_____

_____

_____

_____

_____

_____

_____

_____

_____

_____

© 1995 by John Wiley & Sons, Inc.

Name _____ Date _____

Building Blocks
Prewriting

There are lots of ways to get ideas for stories. One method is to make a list of people, places, and things. These are building blocks for you to juggle around in your mind until they evolve into a story. It will be easy to come up with this list of building blocks if you first answer the following questions: (Write your answers on the line next to each question.)

1. If you could give yourself a new first name, what would it be? _____

2. If you ever have a son, what will you name him? _____

3. If you ever have a daughter, what will you name her? _____

4. If you could travel to any spot on Earth, where would it be? _____

5. If you could travel back in time (or ahead to the future), what year would you choose? _____

6. What is your favorite kind of pet? _____

7. What is your favorite wild animal? _____

8. Where would you hate to be alone in the dark? _____

9. Who or what would you most fear seeing there? _____

10. Where would you like to be right now? _____

11. If you were going on a long journey, how would you prefer to travel (boat, plane, spaceship, horseback, car, and so on)? _____

12. What things do you usually carry in your pocket? _____

13. Name four objects in this room that are larger than a notebook._____

BUILDING YOUR BLOCKS (BRAINSTORMING LIST): Your answers to the above questions can be put together to make a story. First, organize them. Copy your answers next to the appropriate captions on the brainstorming list on the next page.

© 1995 by John Wiley & Sons, Inc.

BRAINSTORMING LIST

Names of characters: _____

When story takes place: _____

Where are characters now? _____

Where do they want to go?_____

How do they want to get there? _____

Who is trying to stop them?_____

What creatures do they meet on the way?_____

What things do they find that help them reach their destination?_____

_____

© 1995 by John Wiley & Sons, Inc.

© 1995 by John Wiley & Sons, Inc.

Name _____ **Date** _____

Building Blocks
First Draft and Group Sharing

DIRECTIONS: Make up a story (no longer than one page) using the information on your brainstorming list in Activity 94A. This is just a guide to get you started—you don't have to follow it exactly. Feel free to change things around, add characters or events, or leave out some items.

Write a first draft of your story below. (Use the back of this paper if you need more room.) This is just a draft; don't worry about spelling or grammar—just concentrate on getting down your thoughts.

_____

_____

_____

_____

_____

_____

_____

GROUP SHARING: Meet with your small group and share your stories. Try to give helpful suggestions, such as:

1. Is there anything that is not clear that the author should explain in more detail?

2. Is the same word used twice in the same sentence or in nearby sentences? What other word would be just as good or even better?

3. Could any of the other language be improved with different words or phrases?

4. Would the writing be clearer if some words were cut?

5. Is it always clear which character is doing what?

6. Can you think of anything to change or add that would make the story more exciting?

Name _____   Date _____

Building Blocks
Revising and Writing a Final Copy

DIRECTIONS: Revise your first draft. First, consider all the suggestions made by your group. If you agree that these will improve the story, make the changes on your copy. Here are some more suggestions:

1. Is your story believable?

2. Do you describe each character? Do they act believably?

3. Is there anything you can change or add that would make the story more exciting and interesting?

4. Do you describe the background where the story takes place?

5. Do you always use the most effective word or phrase? Are there any that can be improved?

6. Are your sentences complete? Do subjects and verbs agree?

    When your story is as good as you can make it, write the final copy below. Make up a title for your story and write it on the first line. (Use the back of this paper if you need more room.)

_____

_____

_____

_____

_____

_____

_____

_____

_____

_____

© 1995 by John Wiley & Sons, Inc.

Name _____ Date _____

Getting More Ideas
Prewriting

Things happen around you all the time that could turn into a plot for a story. All you have to do is add a little imagination. Here is one such situation:

> Jeremy and Nicole Franklin are staying with their Aunt Helen while their parents are on a trip. Aunt Helen lives in an apartment house in a large city. She's great, but there is a large, mean kid named Chuck living in the apartment next door. Chuck is pleasant and polite when adults are around, but whenever he catches Jeremy or Nicole alone, he bullies and teases them. One day, he really hurts Nicole. She and Jeremy decide to get even. They come up with a plan that will teach Chuck a lesson and make him stop bothering them.

This paragraph gives you the basic plot of a story, but you need to know a lot more before you can write it. The brainstorming list below will help you come up with this additional information.

DIRECTIONS: Come up with the additional details you need for your story by answering the questions on the brainstorming list. (You don't need sentences—just words and phrases.)

BRAINSTORMING LIST

How old is Jeremy? What does he look like?_____

_____

How old is Nicole? What does she look like?_____

_____

List some words that describe Jeremy's personality. _____

_____

List some words that describe Nicole's personality._____

_____

Describe Aunt Helen. _____

_____

© 1995 by John Wiley & Sons, Inc.

Describe Chuck. _____

_____

Describe Aunt Helen's apartment house. _____

_____

What city is it in? _____

_____

What things do Jeremy and Nicole like and dislike about the city? _____

_____

What mean things does Chuck do to them? _____

_____

How do they teach Chuck a lesson? _____

_____

© 1995 by John Wiley & Sons, Inc.

Name _____ **Date** _____

Getting More Ideas
First Draft and Group Sharing

DIRECTIONS: Write a first draft of your story about Jeremy and Nicole and the bully, Chuck, on the lines below. Use the plot situation in Activity 95A and the details you worked out on your brainstorming list. This is only a first draft, so don't worry about spelling or grammar. Just concentrate on writing down your thoughts. (Use the back of this paper if you need more room.)

_____

_____

_____

_____

_____

_____

_____

_____

_____

_____

GROUP SHARING: Meet with your small group and share your stories. Try to give helpful suggestions, such as:

1. Is there anything that is not clear that the author must explain in more detail?

2. Are the characters and background described well enough for the reader to see them?

3. Is the plot convincing, especially the part where Jeremy and Nicole teach Chuck a lesson?

4. Would the story be more effective with a word or phrase cut?

5. Can you think of any ways to improve the language with more effective words or phrases?

© 1995 by John Wiley & Sons, Inc.

Name _____ **Date** _____

Getting More Ideas

Revising and Writing a Final Copy

DIRECTIONS: Revise your story about Jeremy and Nicole's week with Aunt Helen in the city. First, consider all the suggestions made by your group. If you agree that these will improve your story, make the changes on your copy. Here are some additional suggestions:

1. Do your characters look and act like real people?

2. Would Jeremy and Nicole's plan to teach Chuck a lesson work in real life? If not, maybe you should change it.

3. Do you have any unnecessary words? If so, take them out.

4. Do you always use the most effective word or phrase? Are there some that can be improved?

5. Are your sentences complete? Do subjects and verbs agree?

When your story is as good as you can make it, write the final copy below. Make up a title and write it on the first line. (Use the back of this paper if you need more room.)

_____

_____

_____

_____

_____

_____

_____

_____

_____

_____

_____

© 1995 by John Wiley & Sons, Inc.

© 1995 by John Wiley & Sons, Inc.

Name _____ **Date** _____

Feeling Fine
Prewriting

Language that appeals to the senses can make your writing more interesting. Sensory words and phrases help the reader *see, hear, smell, taste,* and *feel* what's happening in your story. Read the following paragraph. Then, answer the questions below.

Sara's eyes were sticky. Her whole body ached with fatigue. But she couldn't fall asleep. The ticking of the tiny blue porcelain clock on her table resounded in her ears like the clanging of a huge brass bell. The sheer white curtains at her window fluttered in the breeze. A sweet scent of gardenias drifted through the open window. And beyond the blue-printed wallpaper behind her bed, rough voices erupted in anger. There were loud footsteps, crashing and banging of furniture. Sara pressed her hot, sweaty palms over her ears.

1. List all the words in this paragraph that refer to the sense of sound. _____
_____

2. Can you think of five more sensory/sound words? _____
_____

3. List words in this paragraph that refer to the sense of sight. _____
_____

4. Write at least five more sensory/sight words. _____
_____

5. What words in the paragraph apply to the sense of touch? _____
_____

6. Write at least five more sensory/touch words. _____
_____

7. What words in the paragraph apply to the sense of smell? _____
_____

8. Write at least five more sensory/smell words. _____
_____

9. Are there any words that refer to the sense of taste? _____
_____

10. Write at least five more sensory/taste words. _____
_____

Name _____   **Date** _____

Feeling Fine
First Draft and Group Sharing

DIRECTIONS: Choose one of the following situations to write about. Put a check in the box next to the one you have chosen.

❏ *1.* Four kids playing ball on a beach

❏ *2.* A family walking down a city street

❏ *3.* Two people escaping from a house fire

❏ *4.* A brother and sister baking a cake in their kitchen

❏ *5.* A group of people flying kites in a park

    Write a paragraph (at least six sentences) describing this situation. Give your characters names. Describe the background and tell what happens. Include as many sensory words as you can. There should be at least one in each sentence. This is just a first draft, so don't worry about spelling and grammar.

_____

_____

_____

_____

_____

_____

_____

© 1995 by John Wiley & Sons, Inc.

GROUP SHARING: Meet with your small group and share your paragraphs. Try to give helpful suggestions, such as:

1. Is there anything that is not clear that the author must explain in more detail?

2. Is there at least one sensory word in each sentence? Are these words appropriate and effective?

3. Can you suggest any additional sensory words that would make the paragraph better?

4. Would the paragraph be more effective with a word or phrase cut?

Name _____   **Date** _____

Feeling Fine
Revising and Writing a Final Copy

DIRECTIONS: Revise your first draft. First, consider all the suggestions made by your group. If you agree that these will improve the story, make the changes on your copy. Here are some more suggestions:

1. Do you name and describe your characters and where they are?

2. Do you use a sensory word in each sentence? Can you think of any additional or better sensory words?

3. Is there anything you would like to add or change to make this situation more interesting?

4. Are your sentences complete? Do subjects and verbs agree?

When your paragraph is as good as you can make it, write the final copy below. (Use the back of this paper if you need more room.)

_____

_____

_____

_____

_____

_____

_____

_____

_____

_____

_____

_____

© 1995 by John Wiley & Sons, Inc.

Name _____ Date _____

Leaping and Shouting
Prewriting

He goes there. This is a dull sentence because goes is a dull, passive verb. You can make it more exciting by using an active verb, as in:

He runs there. Or
He hops there. Or
He speeds there.

Here is another boring sentence: He said it. Wouldn't it be better to write:

He shouted it. Or
He whispered it. Or
He hissed it.

DIRECTIONS:

1. Underline the active verbs in the following scene:

Alan jumped onto his bike and sped away down the street.
"Hi!" he yelled, as he raced past his friend Jimmy.
"Watch out!" he shouted, as he narrowly missed crashing into an old lady. Alan shook his head and continued to pump away on the pedals. Suddenly, he braked hard and screeched to a halt. He had almost flown past his destination.

2. Next to each passive verb below are several more exciting, active verbs that could take its place. Can you add at least two or three more active verbs to each listing?

Go:	run, leap,_____
Say:	shout, whisper, _____
See:	stare, squint, _____
Touch:	pat, slap, _____
Eat:	gobble, chew, _____
Take:	snatch, seize, _____

3. Rewrite the paragraph below, changing each underlined passive verb into an active verb.

Jenna left her room and went down the stairs. She went into the kitchen and saw two boxes of cereal on the table. Her brother, Gary, was eating. "Save some for me," Jenna said. She took a bowl from the cupboard.

_____

_____

_____

© 1995 by John Wiley & Sons, Inc.

Name _____ **Date** _____

Leaping and Shouting
First Draft and Group Sharing

DIRECTIONS: Choose one of the following scenes to write about. Check the box next to the one you have chosen. Then write the first draft of a brief story about that situation. Use active verbs wherever possible.

❑ *1.* It is the last inning of a Little League baseball game and the batter thinks that the umpire made a bad call.

❑ *2.* A family is hiking in the woods. One of the kids gets separated from the rest and is lost.

❑ *3.* A kid is walking home from school loaded down with books. Suddenly, it begins to rain hard.

❑ *4.* Two kids have a disagreement in the playground. It turns into a fight.

Write the first draft of a description of the scene you have chosen. Name the characters and tell what happens. Try to use at least four active verbs in your description. (Use the back of this paper if you need more room.)

_____

_____

_____

_____

_____

_____

GROUP SHARING: Meet with your small group and share your descriptions. Try to give helpful suggestions, such as:

1. Does anything sound awkward or unclear?

2. Are the verbs active and exciting? Can you suggest places where additional active verbs would improve the writing?

3. Are there any extra, unnecessary words that could be cut?

© 1995 by John Wiley & Sons, Inc.

Name _____   **Date** _____

Leaping and Shouting
Revising and Writing a Final Copy

DIRECTIONS: Revise your first draft. First, consider the suggestions made by your group. If you agree that these will improve the story, make the changes on your copy. Here are some more suggestions:

1. Can you add any additional active verbs to make the writing more exciting?

2. Is there anything you can change or add that would make the description more exciting and interesting?

3. Do you always use the most effective word or phrase? Are there any that can be improved?

4. Are your sentences complete? Do subjects and verbs agree?

When your description is as good as you can make it, write the final copy below. Make up a title for your story and write it on the first line. (Use the back of this paper if you need more room.)

_____

_____

_____

_____

_____

_____

_____

_____

_____

_____

_____

© 1995 by John Wiley & Sons, Inc.

© 1995 by John Wiley & Sons, Inc.

Name _____   Date _____

Where on Earth?
Prewriting

No story takes place in the middle of nowhere! Any scene is always set in a specific spot. The writer needs to describe this background so that it is clear in the reader's mind. Read the following scene. Then, answer the questions below.

> Samantha rushed through the overgrown path in the woods. "C'mon!" she called to Jennie, "we're almost there."
>
> On the far side of a pond stood a tall, gnarled oak tree. Through its branches, Jennie could discern the outlines of a structure. A wooden structure! A tree house! A few rays of sunlight broke through the opening in the trees and Jennie saw the tree house distinctly. It was in sad shape, old and neglected. The wood was weathered and cracked. The roof had come loose and was hanging in splinters over one side.
>
> "That can't be your tree house!" Jennie exclaimed. "It's too old!"

1. Who are the two characters in this scene? _____

2. What are they doing? _____

3. List some words or phrases that tell where these characters are. _____
_____

4. Where is the tree house? _____

5. List some of the words and phrases that help you get a clear picture of the tree house. _____
_____

6. The writer keeps the action going around the description by telling what the characters are doing and saying. Give one or two examples of sentences or phrases that tell what a character is doing. _____
_____

7. Give one or two examples of sentences or phrases that tell what a character is saying. _____

Name _____   **Date** _____

Where on Earth?
First Draft and Group Sharing

DIRECTIONS: Choose one of the following scenes to write about. Check the box next to the one you have chosen.

❏ *1.* Andy and Mariela are building a sand castle on the beach.

❏ *2.* Tom and Zachary are throwing a basketball on the playground.

❏ *3.* Becky and her mom are sitting in a doctor's waiting room.

❏ *4.* Pat walks into his new classroom for the first time.

Write the first draft of this scene, concentrating on the background. Make your description come to life with vivid language, such as sensory words and active verbs. Weave in some action or conversation to make the scene more interesting. Reread the description in Activity 98A. (Use the back of this paper if you need more room.)

© 1995 by John Wiley & Sons, Inc.

_____

_____

_____

_____

_____

_____

GROUP SHARING: Meet with your small group and share your descriptions. Try to give helpful suggestions, such as:

1. Does anything sound awkward or unclear?

2. Is the scene described vividly enough for the reader to see it mentally? What could be added to make it more real?

3. Do the characters say or do something to complete the scene?

4. Are there any unnecessary words that should be cut?

© 1995 by John Wiley & Sons, Inc.

Name _____ **Date** _____

Where on Earth?
Revising and Writing a Final Copy

DIRECTIONS: Revise your draft. Consider the suggestions made by your group. Use them if they will improve the story. Here are some more suggestions:

1. Can you add any additional details that will make the description more complete?

2. Can your language be more vivid and exciting?

3. Are the characters actively woven into the description?

4. Are your sentences complete? Do subjects and verbs agree?

When you are satisfied with your description, write the final copy below. Make up a title for your scene. Write it on the first line. (Use the back of this paper if you need more room.)

_____

_____

_____

_____

_____

_____

_____

_____

_____

_____

_____

_____

Name _____ **Date** _____

What's Happening?
Prewriting

Have you ever started to write a story and had to give it up because you became confused or didn't know how to continue? This won't happen if you know the plot in advance. It's a good idea to do this in writing. Read the following plot summary, then answer the questions below:

> Twelve-year-old Brian Rogers's family has moved four times in the last six years. He's sick of always being the new kid in class and doesn't even try to make new friends. He stays home alone, playing his guitar and making up songs. The other kids think he's stuck-up and keep away from him. This only makes him angrier and he starts getting into fights at school and on the street. One boy, Kevin, befriends Brian. When Brian learns that Kevin has gone to a party that Brian wasn't invited to, they get into an argument. Brian punches Kevin and stomps off. Afterwards, Brian is lonelier than ever. He realizes he has driven off all the other kids, including his only friend. At the school talent show, he performs a song he has written about a stupid boy who feels sorry for himself and acts like a jerk, then realizes how great the other kids are and how much he really wants their friendship. After the show, some of Brian's classmates, including Kevin, come over to him. This time, he shows his real feelings and knows he will soon have friends.

1. Who is the main character in this story?_____

2. What is his big problem? _____

3. What things happen to make his problem worse? _____

_____

_____

4. When does he begin to understand his problem? _____

5. What special occasion does he choose to take action? _____

6. How does he begin to change things around and solve his problem?_____

_____

7. What occurs early in the story that is used by the main character at the end to solve his problem? _____

_____

8. Where does most of the action take place? _____

© 1995 by John Wiley & Sons, Inc.

Name _____ **Date** _____

What's Happening?
First Draft and Group Sharing

DIRECTIONS: Write the first draft of a plot summary for a story of your own or make up a story based on one of the following situations. Check the box next to the one you have chosen.

❑ *1.* Tommy is walking his family dog, Frisky. He stops to talk to a friend. The dog gets loose and runs away.

❑ *2.* Wendy's mom gets remarried. Wendy likes her new stepdad, but she hates her stepbrother, Alan, who lives with them.

❑ *3.* On a camping trip with the Boy Scouts, Joey gets lost. He has to spend two nights and two days alone in the woods before being found.

❑ *4.* There are a series of burglaries on Center Street. Twelve-year-old Ted and his ten-year-old sister, Megan, investigate and discover who is committing these crimes.

❑ *5.* Fourteen-year-old Mar becomes ruler of Planet Anthax when his father is killed by their evil enemy, Thon. He has to defend his land against the forces of Thon, who wants to take over.

Make up additional characters and events to expand these situations into a story. Your plot summary should tell the story from beginning to end. Be brief. Just outline what happens. Save the details for the story itself. Write your first draft of this plot summary below.

_____

_____

_____

_____

_____

_____

GROUP SHARING: Meet with your small group and share your plot summaries. Try to give helpful suggestions, such as:

1. Are the main characters and the problem clearly shown?

2. Does the story hold together? Is there anything that doesn't make sense?

3. Is anything important left out?

4. Are there any unnecessary details that could be cut?

© 1995 by John Wiley & Sons, Inc.

Name _____ Date _____

What's Happening?
Revising and Writing a Final Copy

DIRECTIONS: Revise the first draft of your plot summary. Consider the suggestions made by your group. Here are some more things to look for:

1. Is the plot believable?

2. Is there a problem that is clearly stated?

3. Does the end make sense based on what comes before?

4. Does each character serve a purpose in the story?

5. Is there a definite main character?

6. Is anything left out that is important to the plot?

7. Are there any unnecessary details that don't belong in the plot summary?

   Write the final copy of your plot summary below. Make up a title for your story and write it on the first line. (Use the back of this paper if you need more room.)

_____

_____

_____

_____

_____

_____

_____

_____

_____

_____

_____

© 1995 by John Wiley & Sons, Inc.

100A

Name _____ Date _____

Who Are You?
Prewriting

It's fun to make up characters for stories! You can decide what they're going to look like, what kind of personalities they'll have, and how they will act in the story. There are several ways you can make your character seem real.

First, of course, you want to describe the character's physical appearance. It can be even more interesting if you include descriptions of his or her way of dressing, mannerisms (ways of walking, standing, touching, smiling, and so on), and speech. This can often tell you something about the individual's personality and character, too.

Read the following example and answer the questions below.

The door opened and Madame Sophie swept in. Madame Sophie never just came into a room. She always made an entrance! It was impossible not to notice Madame Sophie. She was quite tall, of regal bearing, and seemed even taller as a result of her erect posture and the imperious manner in which she held her head. Her blond hair, streaked with silver, was piled into a complicated twist at the top of her head. Although most of her dancing now was confined to teaching, her body was still strong and supple. She wore leotards and tights, and her muscular dancer's legs were covered with woolen wrappers.

1. List three phrases that tell something about Madame Sophie's physical appearance. __
   _____
   _____
   _____

2. What is she wearing? _____

3. What does her way of dressing tell you about her?_____

4. List two or three mannerisms that Madame Sophie has. _____
   _____
   _____
   _____

5. What do these tell you about her personality?_____

6. Can you find at least three sensory words that help make this description vivid? _____
   _____

7. Can you find at least three active verbs that help make this description come alive? __
   _____

Name _____ **Date** _____

Who Are You?
First Draft and Group Sharing

DIRECTIONS: Write the first draft of a description of one of the following. Check the box next to the one you have chosen.

❑ *1.* One of the characters from the plot summary you wrote for Activity 99B

❑ *2.* A character from another story you have written or may write

❑ *3.* The grown-up man or woman you hope to be one day

❑ *4.* One of your favorite characters on TV

❑ *5.* Someone in your family

❑ *6.* One of your friends

Be sure to include the following:

1. Use sensory words and other vivid language in your physical description.

2. Describe mannerisms, such as ways of walking, talking, and moving that use active verbs.

3. Show how the character dresses.

4. Show some personality traits.

5. Give your character a name, unless there is some reason not to do so.

Write your first draft below. Then, share it with your small group, if one is available. (Use the back of this paper is you need more room.)

_____

_____

_____

_____

_____

_____

© 1995 by John Wiley & Sons, Inc.

Name _____   **Date** _____

Who Are You?
Revising and Writing a Final Copy

DIRECTIONS: Revise your first draft. Here are some suggestions:

1. Can you add any additional details about the character's appearance?

2. Do your character's mannerisms and dress tell something about his or her personality?

3. Can any of the language be more vivid and exciting? Can you add more sensory words and active verbs?

4. Have you used any words or phrases more than once? If so, substitute another word or phrase.

5. Are your sentences complete? Do subjects and verbs agree?

When you are satisfied with your character description, write the final copy below. (Use the back of this paper if you need more room.)

_____

_____

_____

_____

_____

_____

_____

_____

_____

_____

_____

_____

© 1995 by John Wiley & Sons, Inc.

Name _____ **Date** _____

Say What?
Prewriting

Do you like to read books that have a lot of dialogue? Most people do. Writing dialogue can be easy, if you understand the rules.

The reader must always know who is speaking. Sometimes the writer fails to indicate the speaker, as in the following example:

> "Come here," Mary said.
> "No, I won't!"
> "Why not."
> "I don't have to tell you."
> "Yes, you do."
> "I'm leaving."

Dialogue like this confuses the reader. It's not necessary to identify the speaker every single time, only often enough to make it clear *who* is saying *what*. You don't want to repeat the word *said* over and over again, but you can use substitutes that are even better such as yelled, whispered, screamed, roared, stuttered, and other active verbs. Can you rewrite the dialogue above, showing who is speaking without overusing *said*?

_____

_____

_____

_____

© 1995 by John Wiley & Sons, Inc.

Dialogue is more effective when it shows time, action, place, or character. The dialogue can be woven in with action and description to create a more vivid and realistic scene. Read the following scene containing dialogue, then answer the questions on the next page.

> "It's a bad sprain. I'm afraid you're going to be hobbling around for a few weeks," said the doctor, as he taped Ellen's foot and ankle.
> "A few weeks! But I must be able to dance by next week!" cried Ellen.
> The doctor shook his head. "Impossible," he told Ellen in a gentle but firm tone that left no room for doubt.
> "Oh, Mom!" Ellen cried after the doctor had left. "What will I do? Next Monday is the day that Madame Sophie announces her decision. I'm supposed to dance for her."
> Mrs. Stone hugged her daughter sympathetically. "I'm sorry, dear, but there's nothing to be done."
> Ellen was inconsolable. "It's all my fault!" she wailed. "I did it to myself. I was careless." She turned away.

1. What words or phrases show action? _____

_____

2. What words or phrases show time? _____

_____

3. What words or phrases show character or feelings? _____

_____

© 1995 by John Wiley & Sons, Inc.

Name _____ **Date** _____

Say What?
First Draft and Group Sharing

DIRECTIONS: Read the dialogue below.

> Mike saw Andy. "Hi," he said.
> "Hi," Andy replied.
> "Are you ready?"
> "Yeah. Are you?"
> "Okay. Let's get started"
> Andy was all set. So was Mike.

The reader can't always be sure *who* is saying *what* in this dialogue. It is also boring because the writer did not give any sense of action, time, place, or character. Look at the example in Activity 101A and note how these things are woven into that dialogue.

You are going to rewrite the above dialogue about Mike and Andy, adding material that will make it more interesting. It will be helpful to think about some of the following questions:

1. Who is Mike? Who is Andy? What do they look like? What words can you use to describe their appearance and character?

2. Where is this scene taking place? What vivid words can you use to describe the background?

3. What is Mike doing during this conversation? What is Andy doing? What active verbs can be used to describe these actions?

4. What is the scene about? Where are Mike and Andy coming from? Where are they going? Why do they want to go there?

After you have answered these questions in your mind, you will have a clearer picture of the scene to be built around the dialogue. Sometimes it helps to think of it as a scene from a movie or TV program. Get the scene set in your mind. See who these kids are, where they are, and what they are doing, and you'll find it easy to rewrite this dialogue, turning it into an interesting scene.

Write your first draft below. Then, share it with your small group, if one is available. (Use the back of the paper if you need more room.)

_____

_____

_____

_____

© 1995 by John Wiley & Sons, Inc.

Name _____   **Date** _____

Say What?
Revising and Writing a Final Copy

DIRECTIONS: Revise the first draft of your scene with dialogue. Here are some suggestions for making it better.

1. Do you tell enough about Mike and Andy so that the reader can see them clearly?

2. Do you show enough things happening while they are talking? Can you add more strong, active verbs to describe this action?

3. Do you show where this conversation is taking place?

4. Do you indicate something about why this conversation is taking place? Where are they coming from? Where are they going? Why?

5. Is there any way you can make the language more vivid and exciting?

6. Are your sentences complete? Do subjects and verbs agree?

Write the final copy of your scene with dialogue below. This scene could be part of a story. Make up a title for that story and write it on the first line. (Use the back of this paper if you need more room.)

_____

_____

_____

_____

_____

_____

_____

_____

_____

_____

© 1995 by John Wiley & Sons, Inc.

Name _____ **Date** _____

Irresistible Beginnings
Prewriting

A story should grab the reader's interest right away! If you start reading a story that sounds boring, you close the book and look for something else. Right? That's why beginnings are so important.

Here are two beginnings for the same story. Decide which one is better. Then, answer the questions below.

BEGINNING #1

"You should run for president, Erica."

"Mm . . . m," Erica mumbled, not really hearing what Pam was saying. Erica's attention centered on the long-division problem she was trying to work out. She couldn't decide where to place the decimal.

"I mean it, Erica! You could win easily!"

"Win what?" Erica's mind was still fixed on the math problem.

"You should run for president of sixth-grade class."

BEGINNING #2

Erica and Pam were doing their homework. They were in Erica's room in her house on Center Street. Erica's room was on the third floor. It was a small room with a bed, a chest, and a desk. There were two windows and a lamp on the desk. Erica and Pam were working on their math assignments. They had 20 problems to do for homework. There were five problems in division, ten in multiplication, and five with fractions. The problems were really hard, so Erica didn't think they had much time for talking.

1. Which beginning uses dialogue? _____

2. Which beginning has more active verbs? _____ Name some of them. _____
_____

3. Which beginning presents an exciting situation right away?_____

4. What is that situation?_____

5. How does the use of dialogue create interest? _____
_____

6. What does Beginning #1 show you about the characters right away?_____
_____

7. How does it do this? _____

8. What details in Beginning #2 are boring and should be cut?_____
_____

© 1995 by John Wiley & Sons, Inc.

Name _____   **Date** _____

Irresistible Beginnings
First Draft and Group Sharing

DIRECTIONS: Write the first draft of a beginning for one of the following story ideas. Check the box next to the one you have chosen.

❏ *1.* Two kids go trick-or-treating on Halloween and find a real haunted house.

❏ *2.* Elena wants to be accepted by the popular group at school. They are all rich and well-dressed. She is poor and wears hand-me-downs.

❏ *3.* Mike's best friend, Bobby, is always getting into trouble. Now, Mike finds himself getting into trouble, too.

❏ *4.* The Hot Peppers Little League team is getting ready for a championship game with their rivals, the Red Devils. The Devils always win by using dirty tricks. How can the Peppers play honestly and still win the game?

❏ *5.* Wendy and Greg's mom has remarried. The kids believe their stepfather is a spy.

❏ *6.* Any story idea of your own.

Write a first draft of a beginning for your story below. Then, share it with your small group, if you have one. Try to grab the reader's interest with vivid language, an exciting situation, and perhaps some dialogue. Remember, this is only the beginning of the story—no more than 12 lines.

_____

_____

_____

_____

_____

_____

_____

_____

_____

© 1995 by John Wiley & Sons, Inc.

© 1995 by John Wiley & Sons, Inc.

Name _____ **Date** _____

Irresistible Beginnings
Revising and Writing a Final Copy

DIRECTIONS: Revise the first draft of your story beginning. Here are some suggestions:

1. Do you show something about the characters right away?

2. Do you introduce an exciting situation or problem?

3. Do you use enough dialogue to stimulate interest?

4. Do you show enough action?

5. Can you make the language more vivid and exciting with active verbs or sensory words?

6. Are your sentences complete? Do subjects and verbs agree?

Write the final copy of your beginning below. Make up a title for the story and write it on the first line. (Use the back of this paper if you need more room.)

_____

_____

_____

_____

_____

_____

_____

_____

_____

_____

_____

_____

Name _____ Date _____

A Day in the Life of the Sillies
Prewriting

© 1995 by John Wiley & Sons, Inc.

The Sillies are a family. They live in the city of Non Sense on the planet Funni.
Who is in the Sillie family? What do they do? Well, that's for you to decide. You are going to write a story about this far-out, foolish family. First, you will use this prewriting worksheet to come up with ideas. After you answer the questions, you'll know a lot about your characters and what happens to them.

1. How many people are there in your Sillie family? _____

2. At the beginning of each line below, write the name of one of the Sillies. Next to each name, list words and phrases that describe this character (appearance, personality, habits, likes and dislikes, position in family, and so on). Begin with Mr. Sillie, the father. _____
_____
_____
_____
_____
_____

3. What other characters will appear in your story? Write each one's name at the beginning of a line, then describe who they are, what they look and act like, and what they have to do with the Sillies. _____
_____
_____
_____
_____

4. List words and phrases that can be used in your description of the Sillies's home. ____
_____

5. List words and phrases that can be used in your description of the city Non Sense. ___
_____

6. List words and phrases that can be used in your description of the planet Funni. ___
_____

7. Write a short plot summary, outlining what's going to happen in your story. (Use the back of this paper if you need more room.) _____
_____
_____
_____
_____

Name _____ **Date** _____

A Day in the Life of the Sillies
First Draft and Group Sharing

DIRECTIONS: Write the first draft of a story called "A Day in the Life of the Sillies." Use the ideas on your prewriting worksheet. Here are some hints on how to write a better story:

1. Make your beginning exciting.

2. Use some dialogue.

3. Describe your characters. Also show what they're like by what they do and say.

4. Tell something about the background (where they are).

5. Use vivid language, such as active verbs and sensory words.

6. Use your plot summary as a guide.

Write a first draft of your story below. Indent at the beginning of each paragraph. Use the back of this paper if you need more room. Then share it with your small group if you have one.

A DAY IN THE LIFE OF THE SILLIES

_____

_____

_____

_____

_____

_____

_____

_____

_____

_____

© 1995 by John Wiley & Sons, Inc.

Name _____ **Date** _____

A Day in the Life of the Sillies
Revising and Writing a Final Copy

DIRECTIONS: Revise the first draft of your story, as follows:

1. Is each character clearly described?

2. Is the background clearly described?

3. Is your beginning exciting enough?

4. Is your plot clear and definite?

5. Can your language be more vivid and exciting?

6. Can you cut out unnecessary or repeated words?

7. Are your sentences complete? Do subjects and verbs agree?

Write the final copy of your story below.

A DAY IN THE LIFE OF THE SILLIES

_____

_____

_____

_____

_____

_____

_____

_____

_____

_____

_____

© 1995 by John Wiley & Sons, Inc.

UNIT EIGHT

Variety Pack

This unit contains an assortment of writing projects. Included is poetry, journal writing, journalism, stream of consciousness, and so on. The steps of the writing process are used wherever possible. However, some of the activities are designed to encourage free, untrammeled expression. A pragmatic, analytical approach such as the writing process would not and should not be appropriate in these cases.

Small-group critiquing can be extremely helpful, particularly with poetry or journalism. A lot can be learned from hearing or reading other people's articles or poetry. No student, however, should ever be compelled to share private thoughts, and group meetings are best omitted from activities in journal writing, stream of consciousness, and some poetry.

Although each of these activities has a specific educational purpose, they are directed at student interest and involvement. Most students will be able to follow the clear, simple directions on their own with a minimum of teacher explanation.

© 1995 by John Wiley & Sons, Inc.

Name _____ Date _____

Rhyme Time
Prewriting

RHYMING WORDS: Rhyming words can be fun, as in *sunny/funny, talk/walk, handle/candle, may/say*. Can you think of at least three words that rhyme with each of the following? Write your rhyming words on the line next to each word.

run _____   faking _____

day _____   snake _____

seat _____

Rhyming words can be spelled differently, as in *staff/laugh/graph* and *true/through/grew*. Can you think of a rhyme that is spelled differently for each of the following words?

neigh _____   lane _____

head _____   weigh _____

bored _____   guessed _____

RHYMED COUPLETS: *Couplet* means two lines. In a *rhymed couplet*, the last word on each line rhymes. Rhymed couplets are fun and easy to write. They are used a lot in popular songs, such as rap, and even in older folk songs. Here are some well-known couplets:

> *"Down in the valley, the valley so <u>low</u>,*
> *Hang your head over, hear the wind <u>blow</u>."*

> *"Twinkle, twinkle, little <u>star</u>,*
> *How I wonder what you <u>are</u>."*

> *"Oh, I wish I was in the land of <u>cotton</u>,*
> *Old times there are ne'er <u>forgotten</u>."*

Many poems use rhymed couplets, as in:

> *"What are you able to build with your <u>blocks</u>?*
> *Castles and palaces, temples and <u>docks</u>."* (R.L. Stevenson)

> *"Brown and <u>furry</u>*
> *Caterpillar in a <u>hurry</u>."*   (Christina Rossetti)

Can you complete each couplet below with a rhyming word?

I love to see
The fish in the _____.

One cold, starry night
I saw a great _____

The fish like to eat
All that they _____

Birds can spread their wings and fly
We must stay on Earth and _____

© 1995 by John Wiley & Sons, Inc.

Name _____ **Date** _____

Rhyme Time
First Draft

A group of couplets can be put together to make a complete song or poem, as in this example:

"Brown and furry
Caterpillar in a hurry;

Take your walk
To the shady leaf or stalk.

May no toad spy you
May the little birds pass by you;

Spin and die,
To live again a butterfly."   (Christina Rossetti)

This is a poem about a caterpillar. Can you put a group of couplets together to make a poem or song about a living thing? It can be about a small creature (like the caterpillar); or about an animal, bird, or reptile; or about an imaginary creature that exists only in your mind. Here are some examples of beginning couplets:

A lion living in the zoo
Is not as free as me or you."

'The eagle is so huge and proud
It soars as high as any cloud."

"I have a secret, hidden spot
That's where you'll find my ocelot."

"Upon my horse I have no fears
Of winds that whistle past my ears."

© 1995 by John Wiley & Sons, Inc.

DIRECTIONS: Write the first draft of a poem or song consisting of at least four rhymed couplets (eight lines). You can begin with one of the sample couplets on page 278, or make up your own.

_____

_____

_____

_____

_____

_____

_____

© 1995 by John Wiley & Sons, Inc.

Name _____ **Date** _____

Rhyme Time
Revising and Writing a Final Copy

DIRECTIONS: Look over and revise your poem or song of rhymed couplets. Here are some suggestions for improvement:

1. Does the last word in each couplet rhyme?

2. Is the subject of your poem clearly stated?

3. Do you use vivid language, such as active verbs and sensory words?

4. Do you have at least four couplets (eight lines)?

5. Would the poem be improved or more complete if you added another couplet?

When your poem is as good as you can make it, write the final copy below. First, make up a title and write it on the first line.

_____

_____

_____

_____

_____

_____

_____

_____

_____

_____

_____

_____

© 1995 by John Wiley & Sons, Inc.

Name _____ **Date** _____

Flower Power
Prewriting

Poems can create wonderful images. If you wanted to describe a snow scene, you could just write, "*It was snowing over the woods and fields,*" but a poet described it like this:

> "*Out of the bosom of the air*
> *Out of the cloud-folds of her garments shaken,*
> *Over the woodlands brown and bare*
> *Over the harvest-fields forsaken*
> *Silent, and soft, and slow*
> *Descends the snow.*"   (H.W. Longfellow)

The poet made the image vivid and beautiful by using the following:

1. Metaphor. A metaphor is a comparison that describes a thing or act as something it really is not. Common metaphors are "Joe applied for the job, but struck out." *Struck out* is a metaphor here because Joe wasn't really playing baseball. "My little brother is a devil." *Devil* is a metaphor here because the child is not really the devil. One of the metaphors in the above poem is *bosom of the air*. The air does not really have a bosom.

There is another metaphor in the second line of the poem. Can you find it? Write this metaphor here: _____

2. Sensory language. The poet also uses words and phrases that appeal to the five senses (taste, touch, smell, sight, and sound). The word *brown* on the third line refers to the sense of sight. There are several other sensory words in this poem. Find them and copy them here: _____

3. Active verbs are strong action words such as *run* instead of *go*, or *shout* instead of *say*. *Shaken* on the second line of the poem is an active verb. Can you find any others? Write them here: _____

Here is a poem that describes water snakes swimming near a ship.

> "*Beyond the shadow of the ship,*
> *I watched the water-snakes:*
> *They moved in tracks of shining white,*
> *And when they reared, the elfish light*
> *Fell off in hoary flakes.*
> *Within the shadow of the ship*
> *I watched their rich attire:*
> *Blue, glossy green, and velvet black,*
> *They coiled and swam; and every track*
> *Was a flash of golden fire.*"   (S.T. Coleridge)

© 1995 by John Wiley & Sons, Inc.

Can you find the metaphors, sensory words, and active verbs in the poem on the previous page? Write them on the lines below.

Metaphors: _____

_____

Sensory words: _____

_____

Active verbs: _____

_____

© 1995 by John Wiley & Sons, Inc.

Name _____   **Date** _____

Flower Power
First Draft and Small-Group Sharing

DIRECTIONS: Reread the poems on the prewriting activity sheet. Examine the way the poets used language to create vivid images. Look at the metaphors, sensory words, and active verbs.

You can use the same language techniques to create your own poem. Choose one of the following subjects to describe in a poem. Check the box next to the one you have chosen.

❑ *1.* An evening with a full moon and a sky filled with stars

❑ *2.* A stadium at the end of a baseball or football game

❑ *3.* The house in which you live

❑ *4.* A beach or park you have visited

❑ *5.* A bike ride

❑ *6.* A Halloween evening

❑ *7.* Any other scene or activity of your choice

Before writing the poem, first list on the lines below words and phrases that can be used in your poem.

Metaphors: _____

Sensory words: _____

Active verbs: _____

Other vivid words and phrases: _____

Now, write the first draft of your poem. You may use rhyme, as in the examples on the prewriting worksheet, but you don't have to use rhyme if you can write a better poem without it. Your poem should be at least six lines long.

_____

_____

_____

_____

_____

_____

© 1995 by John Wiley & Sons, Inc.

SMALL-GROUP SHARING: Share the poems written by your group. Make suggestions for improvement, such as:

1. Should anything be added to make the scene more vivid?

2. Should anything be taken out to make it more effective?

3. Can you suggest stronger words and phrases to replace weak ones?

4. Can you suggest changes that would make the poem flow more rhythmically?

© 1995 by John Wiley & Sons, Inc.

Name _____   **Date** _____

Flower Power
Revising and Writing a Final Copy

DIRECTIONS: Revise your descriptive poem, as follows:

1. Do you feel a sense of rhythm when you read the poem aloud?

2. Have you used at least one metaphor? If not, add one now.

3. Have you used at least three sensory words? If not, add some now.

4. Have you used at least two active verbs? If not, add them now.

5. Are there any weak or boring words in your poem? Take them out or replace them with more vivid language.

6. Would your description be better and more complete if you added a few more lines? If so, add them now.

7. Are there any words or phrases that are unnecessary because they add nothing to the description? If so, take them out.

    When your poem is as good as you can make it, write your final copy on the lines below. First, make up a title and write it on the first line. If you like, you can also illustrate your poem in the box below.

_____

_____

_____

_____

_____

_____

_____

© 1995 by John Wiley & Sons, Inc.

Name _____ Date _____

What's It Like?
Prewriting

It can be fun to describe something by comparing it to something else, as in:

"Out of the night that covers me,
Black as the pit from pole to pole."

"The wild tulip, at end of its tube, blows out its great red bell
Like a thin clear bubble of blood."

"There's nothing to see but a cushion of snow
Round as a pillow, and whiter than milk."

The first two lines compare the *night* to a *black pit*. The next compares the *red part of a tulip* to *blood*. The last comparison shows a *snow pile* to be *round* like a *pillow* and *white* like *milk*.

EXERCISE A—DIRECTIONS: Complete the following lines with interesting comparisons:

1. My puppy's hair is like _____

2. My mom's voice is like _____

3. Stevie is as wild as _____

4. Her face was as white as _____

The poet Christina Rossetti found three things to compare to her heart in this poem entitled, "A Birthday."

"My heart is like a singing bird
Whose nest is in a water'd shoot;
My heart is like an apple-tree
Whose boughs are bent with thick-set fruit;
My heart is like a rainbow shell
That paddles in a halcyon sea;"

© 1995 by John Wiley & Sons, Inc.

EXERCISE B—DIRECTIONS: Can you compare each object below to three things? List your comparisons on the line next to each word.

1. Blue eyes _____

2. A frightened child _____

3. The color green _____

4. A cloud _____

5. A football player _____

6. A bad sunburn _____

© 1995 by John Wiley & Sons, Inc.

Name _____ **Date** _____

What's It Like?
First Draft and Small-Group Sharing

DIRECTIONS: Read the poem by Christina Rossetti on your prewriting activity work-sheet in which she makes three different comparisons of her heart. Then look at Exercise B where you wrote down three comparisons for each subject. You are going to choose one of these subjects and write a poem using all three of your comparison ideas. Here is an example of a poem about blue eyes:

"My mother's eyes are deep, deep blue
Like the noon-time sky on a sunny day;
As blue as the sparkling mountain lake
Where we swim on summer afternoons;
As blue as the flowered wallpaper
In my baby brother's room."

On the line below, write down the subject you have chosen. (For example, a football player, or the color green, or a cloud, and so on.)

My subject is _____

You will write at least two lines for each of your comparisons, as in the example above. That will give you a poem of six lines or more. It does not have to rhyme.

Write a first draft of your poem below.

_____

_____

_____

_____

SMALL-GROUP SHARING: Share the poems written by your group. Make suggestions for improvement, such as:

1. Are there any additional comparisons that could be added?

2. Are any words or phrases awkward? How could they be expressed more smoothly?

3. Can you suggest stronger words and phrases to replace weak ones?

4. Are there ways to make the poem flow more rhythmically?

© 1995 by John Wiley & Sons, Inc.

Name _____ **Date** _____

What's It Like?

Revising and Writing a Final Copy

DIRECTIONS: Revise your comparison poem.

1. Do you feel a sense of rhythm when you read the poem aloud? How could you make it flow more smoothly?

2. Have you used at least three comparisons for your subject? Can you add any more?

3. Have you written at least two lines about each comparison?

4. Are there any weak or boring words in your poem? Can you replace them with more vivid language, such as sensory words or active verbs?

When your poem is as good as you can make it, write your final copy on the lines below. First, make up a title and write it on the first line. If you like, you can illustrate your poem in the box below.

_____

_____

_____

_____

_____

_____

_____

_____

© 1995 by John Wiley & Sons, Inc.

Name _____ Date _____

Feeling Happy/Feeling Sad
Prewriting

Poetry can be a good way to express our feelings:

"My heart leaps up when I behold
*   A rainbow in the sky."*

"Deep into that darkness peering, long
*   I stood there wondering, fearing,*
Doubting, dreaming dreams no mortal
*   ever dared to dream before."*

"I was a child and she was a child
*   In this kingdom by the sea;*
But we loved with a love that was more
*   than love—*
I and my Annabel Lee."

My grief on the sea, how the waves of it roll!
For they heave between me and the love of my soul.

Some of these lines are happy. Some are sad. But they all express the writer's feelings.

ASSIGNMENT A—DIRECTIONS: Next to each feeling, write down as many words and phrases as you can think of that might be used to describe that feeling or things that cause that feeling.

Happiness _____

Sadness _____

Fear _____

Anger _____

ASSIGNMENT B—DIRECTIONS: Next to each situation below, make a list of words and phrases that might describe your feelings:

You win first prize in a contest _____

Your best friend moves far away _____

You have a surprise party on your birthday _____

You fail an important test at school _____

© 1995 by John Wiley & Sons, Inc.

© 1995 by John Wiley & Sons, Inc.

Name _____ **Date** _____

Feeling Happy/Feeling Sad
First Draft and Small-Group Sharing

DIRECTIONS: Read the examples on the prewriting activity sheet. Examine the way the poets use language to vividly express their feelings.

You are going to write a poem about feelings. You may describe a feeling, such as sadness, anger, or happiness, or you can write about your feelings at a certain time, in a particular situation, such as those in Assignment B on the prewriting activity sheet. Write your choice on the line below.

_____

Write a poem about this subject. The words and phrases you listed on the prewriting worksheet will help you organize your poem and get started. Can you write at least six lines about your feelings? Your poem does not have to rhyme.

Write a first draft below.

_____

_____

_____

_____

_____

_____

SMALL-GROUP SHARING: Share the poems written by your group. Make suggestions for improvement, such as:

1. Is the feeling expressed by the writer clear? Should anything be added to make it clearer?

2. Can you suggest stronger words or phrases to replace weak ones?

3. Does the poem flow rhythmically? If not, can you suggest changes to improve this?

4. Should anything be added to make the poem stronger?

5. Should anything be taken out to make the poem stronger?

Name _____ **Date** _____

Feeling Happy/Feeling Sad
Revising and Writing a Final Copy

DIRECTIONS: Revise your feelings poem, as follows:

1. Use the suggestions of your small group that you think are helpful.

2. Do you feel a sense of rhythm when you read the poem aloud?

3. Are there any weak or boring words in your poem? Take them out or replace them with more vivid language, such as sensory words, active verbs, similes, or metaphors.

4. Would the expression of your feelings be better and more complete if you added a few more lines? If so, add them now.

   When your poem is as good as you can make it, write your final copy on the lines below. First, make up a title and write it on the first line. If you like, you can also illustrate your poem in the box below.

_____

_____

_____

_____

_____

_____

_____

_____

© 1995 by John Wiley & Sons, Inc.

Name _____ Date _____

Who Am I?
Prewriting

What is a journal? A journal is a place where you can:

- express private thoughts and feelings
- experiment with language; try out different ways of using words and phrases
- write down ideas you may or may not wish to share with others
- learn more about yourself through self-examination
- write to please only yourself

If you decide to keep a journal, you will want to have a special notebook for this purpose—one that you do not have to show to anyone else. These worksheets are just to help you get started. Then you can continue to write in your own journal.

DIRECTIONS: A journal can help you understand yourself better. Begin by completing the following sentences:

1. I feel happy when _____

2. My favorite time of day is _____ because _____
   _____

3. My life would be better if _____
   _____

4. I wish I could be _____

5. I get nervous when _____

6. I am afraid of _____ because _____
   _____

7. Some things I like about my appearance are _____
   _____

8. Some things I don't like about my appearance are _____
   _____

9. I felt sad when _____

10. I got angry when _____

© 1995 by John Wiley & Sons, Inc.

11. I'd rather be at _____ than anywhere else.

12. The things I like to do most are_____

_____

13. My best qualities are _____

_____

14. My biggest fault is _____

15. I think that I am _____

© 1995 by John Wiley & Sons, Inc.

Name _____ **Date** _____

Who Am I?
Final Copy

DIRECTIONS: Use this worksheet to write a journal page describing yourself and how you feel about yourself. The sentences you completed on the prewriting activity sheet can be your guide. But these are just to help you get started. You can add more details or write anything else that comes into your head about who you are. The more details you use, the better your self-picture will be.

You might be surprised how much you can learn about yourself through journal writing.

This activity is for your eyes only. You don't have to show it to anyone else.

A JOURNAL PAGE ABOUT MYSELF

_____
_____
_____
_____
_____
_____
_____
_____
_____
_____
_____
_____
_____
_____

© 1995 by John Wiley & Sons, Inc.

Name _____ **Date** _____

Who Are You?

Prewriting

JOURNAL WRITING

You can learn a lot about yourself by writing in a journal. It can also help you understand other people and your feelings about them. This activity will help get you started.

DIRECTIONS: Complete these sentences. You can be open and honest because you do not have to show your answers to anyone.

1. In my family, I feel closest to my _____ because _____

_____

2. Here is a list of words and phrases that describe that person: _____

_____

3. I think that person is the way he (or she) is because _____

_____

4. I get angry at my _____ when he (or she) _____

_____

5. I think he (or she) acts that way because _____

_____

6. The qualities I like best in a friend are _____

_____

7. I like my friend _____ because _____

_____

8. One thing I don't like about him (or her) is _____

_____

9. We are friends because _____

© 1995 by John Wiley & Sons, Inc.

10. We would not be friends if _____

11. When my friend and I have a disagreement, _____

_____

12. One person I really do not like is _____ because _____

_____

13. I think he (or she) is like that because _____

_____

14. I would like him (or her) better if _____

_____

15. The person I would most want to be like is _____ because _____

_____

© 1995 by John Wiley & Sons, Inc.

Name _____ **Date** _____

Who Are You?
Final Copy

DIRECTIONS: Use this worksheet to write a journal page describing people you know and how you feel about them. The sentences you completed on the prewriting activity sheet can be your guide. These are just to help you get started. You can add a lot more facts about these people and your feelings about them. The more details you use, the better.

You may be surprised to discover that you understand people a lot better after writing about them in your journal.

This activity is for your eyes only. You don't have to show it to anyone else.

A JOURNAL PAGE ABOUT OTHERS

_____

_____

_____

_____

_____

_____

_____

_____

_____

_____

_____

_____

_____

_____

© 1995 by John Wiley & Sons, Inc.

Name _____   **Date** _____

© 1995 by John Wiley & Sons, Inc.

Chasing the News
Prewriting

A reporter writes the news. Most reporters have to do a lot of running about to discover good news stories. You are going to be a lucky reporter. All the facts you need are on this worksheet.

Here are the details about what happened:

1. The police were called to 784 Elm Street on Monday, July 18, at 4:30 P.M.

2. Patrolmen Haynes and Scarletti were let into the house by Martin Stout, age 12.

3. Two young men were locked in a closet on the upper floor. They identified themselves as Gabe Manson and Billy Evans, both 17.

4. Martin told the police officers that he was alone in the house waiting for his parents to return from work when the two teenagers broke in. "They climbed through an upstairs bathroom window," Martin said. He sneaked up behind them, pushed them into the closet, and locked the door. Then he called the police.

5. "We thought the house was empty," Manson said. Evans wouldn't say anything until he saw his lawyer.

6. "This is one brave 12-year-old," said Officer Haynes.

The first few sentences of a news story should answer these questions: *Who? What? When?* and *Where?* The story will be easier to write if you first answer these questions:

1. Who is the main character in this story? _____

2. What happened to him? _____

3. When did it happen? _____

4. Where did it happen? _____

5. Who else was involved? _____

6. What other details are important or interesting? _____

7. What quotations can you use in this story? _____

The beginning of a news story should be exciting enough to make the reader want to read on. Can you think of an interesting first sentence for this news story? It should answer some of these questions: *Who? What? When? Where?* or *Why?* At the same time, it should grab the reader's interest. Write your first sentence below.

Name _____   **Date** _____

Chasing the News
First Draft and Small-Group Sharing

DIRECTIONS: It's time to be a "star reporter" and write the news story described on the prewriting worksheet. Your answers to the questions in that activity will help you write the first draft of your story. Here are some more hints:

1. Be sure your beginning is as interesting and exciting as you can make it.

2. The first few sentences should tell *Who? What? When?* and *Where?*

3. Use some quotations. Be sure to correctly identify the speaker.

Write the first draft of your news story below.

_____

_____

_____

_____

_____

_____

_____

© 1995 by John Wiley & Sons, Inc.

SMALL-GROUP SHARING: Share your news story with your group. Make suggestions for improvement, such as:

1. Does the beginning grab the reader's interest? Can you think of any way to make it more exciting?

2. Do the first few sentences answer these questions: *Who? What? When?* and *Where?*

3. Are any phrases or sentences awkward? How can they be improved?

4. Are there unnecessary words that should be cut?

5. Are there dull words or phrases that could be replaced by more vivid language?

Name _____ **Date** _____

Chasing the News
Revising and Writing a Final Copy

DIRECTIONS: Revise the first draft of your news story.

1. Consider the suggestions made by your group.

2. Is your beginning as exciting as you can make it?

3. Do the first few sentences tell *Who? What? When?* and *Where?*

4. Have you included all important details?

5. Do you clearly identify the speaker when using quotations?

6. Can any of the language be more vivid and exciting? Can you use more sensory words and active verbs?

7. Are your sentences complete? Do subjects and verbs agree?

When you are satisfied with your news story, write the final copy below. If you wish, you can make up a headline, such as "Twelve-Year-Old Boy Nabs Burglars." Write your headline on the first line.

_____

_____

_____

_____

_____

_____

_____

_____

_____

_____

_____

© 1995 by John Wiley & Sons, Inc.

Name _____ **Date** _____

Classroom Flash

Prewriting

You probably think of your classroom as a boring, everyday sort of place, certainly not one where interesting, newsworthy events happen.

If you are a good reporter, however, you will discover that by staying alert and keeping your eyes wide open, you may notice all sorts of situations that could be the basis for exciting news stories. Some journalists call this a *nose for news*.

Here are some things that have happened in ordinary classrooms and were turned into interesting news stories:

An eighth-grade class plans a "junk ecology" drive; it involves collecting egg cartons, soda cans, and other things that can be recycled.

A sixth-grade boy has appeared in several television commercials.

Some seventh-graders are serving on a "safety patrol," watching over third- and fourth-graders as they arrive at school in the mornings and leave in the afternoons.

Two eighth-grade girls have started their own "baby-sitting service." They call it "Sitters on Call."

A substitute music teacher plays regularly with a local rock group.

DIRECTIONS (A): Do you have a *nose for news*? Starting now, watch what goes on in your classroom. Talk to the students and teachers. Can you discover at least three interesting facts or events that would make exciting news stories for your school newspaper? List these three ideas (or more) on the lines below.

❏ _____

❏ _____

❏ _____

DIRECTIONS (B): Choose one of these events to write about. Put a check in the box next to it. Then, on the lines below, list as many facts and details as you can discover about this event. (You don't need sentences—words and phrases are good enough.)

_____

_____

_____

© 1995 by John Wiley & Sons, Inc.

Name _____   Date _____

Classroom Flash
First Draft and Small-Group Sharing

Here is an article that was written for a middle school newspaper:

COMPUTERS IN THE MIDDLE SCHOOL

This year all Middle School students will be required to take a computer course. Room 210 has been set aside for this purpose. There are fourteen Apple computers, each with its own disk drive and monitor, and two printers.

Mr. Roberts will be the instructor. The course is based on a series of workbooks. Each student can move through the books at his or her own rate. Mr. Roberts's goal is to make all students comfortable with computers, aware of what a computer can do, what it is, and how to use it. He calls the course "a program for computer literacy."

Notice how the reporter who wrote this article answered the questions *Who? What? When?* and *Where?* in the first two sentences. The rest of the article goes on to give more details.

DIRECTIONS (A): Write the first few sentences of your article about the event you chose on Activity 111A. Be sure you answer these questions: *Who? What? When?* and *Where?* (This is just a first draft.)

_____

_____

_____

DIRECTIONS (B): Write a first draft of the rest of your article on the lines below. Choose the most important facts to write about first. Put the least important details at the end.

_____

_____

_____

SMALL-GROUP SHARING: Share your news story with your group. Make suggestions for improvement, such as:

1. Do the first few sentences answer these questions: *Who? What? When?* and *Where?*

2. Is there a way to make the beginning more interesting?

3. Are there dull words or phrases that could be more vivid?

4. Are any sentences awkward or incomplete?

© 1995 by John Wiley & Sons, Inc.

Name _____   **Date** _____

Classroom Flash
Revising and Writing a Final Copy

DIRECTIONS: Revise the first draft of your news story.

1. Consider the suggestions made by your group.

2. Does your beginning grab the reader's interest? Is there any way you can make it more exciting?

3. Do the first few sentences tell *Who? What? When?* and *Where?*

4. Have you included all important details?

5. Do you use at least one quotation and clearly identify the speaker?

6. Can any of the language be more vivid and exciting?

7. Are your sentences complete? Do subjects and verbs agree?

When you are satisfied that your news story is as good as you can make it, write the final copy below. Make up a headline and write it on the first line.

_____

_____

_____

_____

_____

_____

_____

_____

_____

_____

© 1995 by John Wiley & Sons, Inc.

Name _____ **Date** _____

An Interview With _Who_?

Prewriting

It's easy to write an interview article. You can include interesting and surprising facts about the subject. This could be a well-known person, such as the mayor of your town, or someone less well-known, such as your school custodian or next-door neighbor.

When you interview a real person, you must be factual. But what if it is not a real, live person? In that case, you can use your imagination to create something different and exciting.

For this activity, you are going to make up an interview with one of the following:

1. a historical figure from the past (such as Abraham Lincoln, Alexander the Great, Christopher Columbus, Babe Ruth, and so on)

2. a fictional character from a book, TV, comic strip, or movie

DIRECTIONS (A): On the line below, write the name of the historical or fictional character you have chosen.

_____

DIRECTIONS (B): Prepare a list of five questions to ask in your "interview." On the lines below each question, write the answers that your subject might give. Try to make your questions and answers as interesting, exciting, and surprising as possible.

1. _____

ANSWER: _____

2. _____

ANSWER: _____

3. _____

ANSWER: _____

4. _____

ANSWER: _____

5. _____

ANSWER: _____

© 1995 by John Wiley & Sons, Inc.

Name _____ **Date** _____

An Interview With Who?
First Draft and Small-Group Sharing

Here is an interview article that was in a school newspaper.

"A friend is someone who is kind, friendly, not a snob, and has a brain." This is what Andrew Cavello looks for in a pal.

Andrew was born in Orange, New Jersey, and is the youngest of three brothers. In his spare time, he likes to play sports, watch TV, go bike riding, or just "hang out." His favorite school subjects are math and reading. When asked what he'd change about school, he replied, "The food . . . ummm . . . less homework . . . and air conditioning."

Andrew's goals for the future are to own a sports car, go to college, and become a dentist or computer programmer.

Notice how the reporter who wrote this article uses quotes to make it livelier and more interesting. Notice also how he organizes the information: family facts, then interests and hobbies, then feelings about school, and then future goals.

DIRECTIONS (A): Look at the questions and answers you prepared for Activity 112A. Choose something unusual or exciting for the beginning of your article. Write this beginning below.

_____

_____

DIRECTIONS (B): Write a first draft of the rest of your interview below. Organize the facts logically, as in the example.

_____

_____

_____

_____

SMALL-GROUP SHARING: Share your interview with your group and make suggestions for improvement, such as:

1. Do the first few sentences identify the subject in an interesting and catchy manner?

2. Are there dull words or phrases that could be more vivid?

3. Are any sentences awkward or incomplete?

4. Is the information organized clearly?

© 1995 by John Wiley & Sons, Inc.

Name _____   **Date** _____

An Interview With Who?
Revising and Writing a Final Copy

DIRECTIONS: Revise the first draft of your news story.

1. Consider the suggestions made by your group.

2. Does your beginning identify the subject and catch the reader's interest?

3. Do you include some interesting quotes?

4. Can you make the language more vivid by using sensory words, similes, or active verbs?

5. Are your sentences complete? Do subjects and verbs agree?

6. Are your facts clearly and logically organized?

When you are satisfied that your interview article is as good as you can make it, write the final copy below. Make up a headline and write it on the first line.

_____

_____

_____

_____

_____

_____

_____

_____

_____

_____

_____

_____

© 1995 by John Wiley & Sons, Inc.

Name _____   Date _____

Strings of Words

Did you ever sit down to write something and a wall went up between your pen and your brain? A complete blank?

Most people experience such blocks from time to time. Usually, it's because you're unsure of yourself or just not comfortable with what you are writing. Whatever the reason, there are ways of breaking through that block. This activity will show you one method to tear down that solid brick wall of resistance. It's also fun!

DIRECTIONS: On the lines below, you are going to write, nonstop, whatever thoughts, words, and ideas come into your head. It doesn't have to be grammatically correct. You don't need correct spelling, punctuation, or complete sentences. (Of course, if you wish to write precisely and grammatically, there's nothing wrong with that!) The idea is to keep writing, no matter what. If you can't think of anything at all, write just that: "I can't think of anything to write." Any kind of nonsense is okay. No one but you will see this.

The important thing is to keep your pen moving until you finish the last line. Once you begin, do not stop for any reason.

This exercise is sometimes called "stream-of-consciousness writing" or "automatic writing."

Okay. Ready to have fun? Begin!

© 1995 by John Wiley & Sons, Inc.

_____

_____

_____

_____

_____

_____

_____

_____

_____

_____

© 1995 by John Wiley & Sons, Inc.

Name _____   **Date** _____

More Strings

Here is another activity that will help break a writing block. It's even easier to do than the one in Activity 113, "Strings of Words."

Sometimes, if a writer is blocked, it's hard to even find that first word you need to begin. In this stream-of-consciousness activity, the first word or the first few words are given to you. You just have to go on from there.

DIRECTIONS: Each section below already has a beginning. Just continue and keep writing until you reach the end. Remember, once you start writing, do not stop for any reason until you reach the end of that section.

SECTION A: I see _____

_____

_____

_____

_____

SECTION B: This is _____

_____

_____

_____

_____

SECTION C: Tomorrow _____

_____

_____

_____

_____

Printed and bound by CPI Group (UK) Ltd, Croydon, CR0 4YY

09/06/2025

14685917-0002